Poems of Hope and Courage

Poems of Hope and Courage

Edited by Ana Sampson

Rizzoli Universe

Published in 2026 by
Rizzoli Universe, a division of
Rizzoli International Publications

Rizzoli International Publications Inc
49 West 27th Street
New York, NY 10001

Rizzoli International Publications UK Ltd
Somerset House, West Wing
Strand, London WC2R 1LA

www.rizzoliusa.com

Publisher: Charles Miers
Associate Publisher: Tina Persaud
Senior Editor: Kristy Richardson
Design: Sarah Pyke
Reproduction: Rival
Production Manager: Michelle Wells

A CIP catalogue record for this book is available from the British Library.

ISBN: 9780789346766

MIX
Paper | Supporting responsible forestry
FSC
www.fsc.org
FSC® C005748

2026 / 1

Printed in China

The authorized representative in the EU for safety and compliance is Mondadori Libri S.p.A., via Gian Battista Vico 42, Milan, Italy, 20123, www.mondadori.it

Visit us online: Instagram.com/RizzoliBooks
Facebook.com/RizzoliNewYork
Youtube.com/user/RizzoliNY

Contents

Introduction

Life asks a lot of us. Each of us will have times when we need to call upon our courage and summon up hope in our hearts. For the dark days, here are bright words. Let them light your way.

Here are the pep talks we need when putting one foot in front of the other seems an impossible proposition. These poems, such as Jean Ingelow's haunted "Middle Watch of the Night," do not shy away from the long dark night of the soul. When the worries that besiege us gather and grow huge in the shadows, calm a racing heart with words from writers who have felt the night terrors and still found courage enough to face the grey dawn:

"I will fear you, O stars, nevermore."
Jean Ingelow

There are morning poems here, for the sunrises when we need to steel ourselves for the coming day. These verses of encouragement remind us that every journey—whatever the destination—starts with a first brave step. "How high those hills, how far away ..." but "Friend, keep going," exhorts Ruth Collie, who published a poem every day as Wilhelmina Stitch during the early years of the turbulent twentieth century.

Our voyage is sometimes perilous, but though we may be tempest-tossed, we are not helpless. With steady sails unfurled, these poems can give us strength to weather the storm—even when the journey's end is uncertain. Into each life, Longfellow tells us, some rain must fall, but

"If all were sun and never rain,
There'd be no rainbow still."
Christina Rossetti

When we reach for a poem in difficult times, the poet holds out a hand to us. These writers—some of them putting pen to paper hundreds of years ago—are telling us that we are not alone. We are not the first—nor will we be the last—to feel downhearted or discouraged, hopeless or bereft. There is solace in knowing that someone has walked this difficult path before us, and that they have dropped these bright breadcrumbs of comfort. We may feel desolate, but we have company in our struggles.

Poets remind us of those who love and lift us, those whose memories sustain us, and the good people doing good things in the world.

"But if the while I think on thee, dear friend,
All losses are restored and sorrows end."
William Shakespeare

You are not alone. "Love is forever over all." Libraries exist, after all. There have always been people offering welcome and comfort, holding a lamp against the darkness. We can be among their number.

For the days when the struggle is most vicious, when the battle waxes bloody, we may need war-like words. Here is armor to buckle on when we are most in need of bravery.

"Courage, yet! My brother or my sister!"
Walt Whitman

Sometimes courage isn't quiet but needs to roar. There are poems here from the trenches, from the fights for civil and women's rights, and even from the playing fields. When nothing less than a clarion call is required, reach for the poets heading into battle and setting off on perilous quests to stiffen your sinews. When rage must build resilience, "Do not go gentle"!

Other writers here prompt us to draw on the strength within us and raise our own song as a candle against the storm. "Stone walls do not a prison make" if we are able to turn the key to our courage. Taking a moment of reflection in the chaos of life—a moment each of these short poems can grant you—can offer the breathing space in which resilience and resolution can bloom.

"'Tis the set of a soul
That decides its goal,
And not the calm or the strife."
Ella Wheeler Wilcox

So many of these poets find hope and joy in the everyday. The peace of wild things, the wood's embrace and the birds' carols can all spark gladness. The light of a steadfast star can lift our hearts. A cup of tea soothes us. The green glories of spring can impart some of their bold energy to us in our weakest, saddest times. A moment with these poems reminds us to sift our humdrum days for delight, fragments to shore against our ruins.

"Sufficient is it just to live
On such a day as this."
Joseph Seamon Cotter Jr.

In the closing chapter, I've gathered some of my favorite poems about starting again. Whether it be a fresh morning, a new spring season with life bursting from the cold earth, or the first page turned in a new book, these are poems of dawning. The sun always rises.

"Take heart with the day and begin again."
Susan Coolidge

The tunnel must come to an end—although it takes great bravery, sometimes, to believe it. These lionhearted poets fill me with faith. I hope they can do the same for you.

Ana Sampson

CHAPTER ONE

Keep Going

“‘Hope’ is the thing with feathers –
That perches in the soul”

‘Hope’ is the Thing with Feathers
Emily Dickinson

May Night

The spring is fresh and fearless
    And every leaf is new.
The world is brimmed with moonlight,
    The lilac brimmed with dew.
Here in the moving shadows
    I catch my breath and sing—
My heart is fresh and fearless
    And over-brimmed with spring.

by Sara Teasdale

'Hope' is the Thing with Feathers

'Hope' is the thing with feathers –
That perches in the soul –
And sings the tune without the words –
And never stops – at all –

And sweetest – in the Gale – is heard –
And sore must be the storm –
That could abash the little Bird
That kept so many warm –

I've heard it in the chillest land –
And on the strangest Sea –
Yet, never, in Extremity,
It asked a crumb – of Me.

by Emily Dickinson

The Old Astronomer to His Pupil *(extract)*

Though my soul may set in darkness, it will rise in perfect light;
I have loved the stars too fondly to be fearful of the night.

by Sarah Williams

To His Heart, Bidding it Have No Fear

Be you still, be you still, trembling heart;
Remember the wisdom out of the old days:
Him who trembles before the flame and the flood,
And the winds that blow through the starry ways,
Let the starry winds and the flame and the flood
Cover over and hide, for he has no part
With the lonely, majestical multitude.

by W. B. Yeats

The Middle Watch of the Night *(extract)*

I will fear you, O STARS, nevermore.

I have felt it! Go on, while the world is ASLEEP,

Golden islands fast moored in God's INFINITE DEEP,

HARK, HARK, to the words of sweet fashion,

the HARPINGS of yore!

by Jean Ingelow

Prayer *(extract)*

Give me the moon at my feet
Put my feet upon the crescent, like a Lord!
O let my ankles be bathed in moonlight, that I may go
sure and moon-shod, cool and bright-footed
towards my goal.

by D. H. Lawrence

Love is Enough

Love is enough: though the World be a-waning,
And the woods have no voice but the voice of complaining,
    Though the sky be too dark for dim eyes to discover
The gold-cups and daisies fair blooming thereunder;
Though the hills be held shadows, and the sea a dark wonder
    And this day draw a veil over all deeds passed over,
Yet their hands shall not tremble, their feet shall not falter;
The void shall not weary, the fear shall not alter
    These lips and these eyes of the loved and the lover.

by William Morris

Who Goes with Fergus?

Who will go drive with Fergus now,
And pierce the deep wood's woven shade,
And dance upon the level shore?
Young man, lift up your russet brow,
And lift your tender eyelids, maid,
And brood on hopes and fear no more.

And no more turn aside and brood
Upon love's bitter mystery;
For Fergus rules the brazen cars,
And rules the shadows of the wood,
And the white breast of the dim sea
And all dishevelled wandering stars.

by W. B. Yeats

Dreams

HOLD FAST TO DREAMS
For if dreams die
Life is a broken-winged bird
That cannot fly.

HOLD FAST TO DREAMS
For when dreams go
Life is a barren field
Frozen with snow.

by Langston Hughes

The Tempest, Act III, Scene II *(extract)*

Be not afeard. The isle is full of noises,
Sounds and sweet airs that give delight and hurt not.
Sometimes a thousand twangling instruments
Will hum about mine ears, and sometime voices
That, if I then had waked after long sleep,
Will make me sleep again; and then, in dreaming,
The clouds methought would open and show riches
Ready to drop upon me, that when I waked
I cried to dream again.

by William Shakespeare

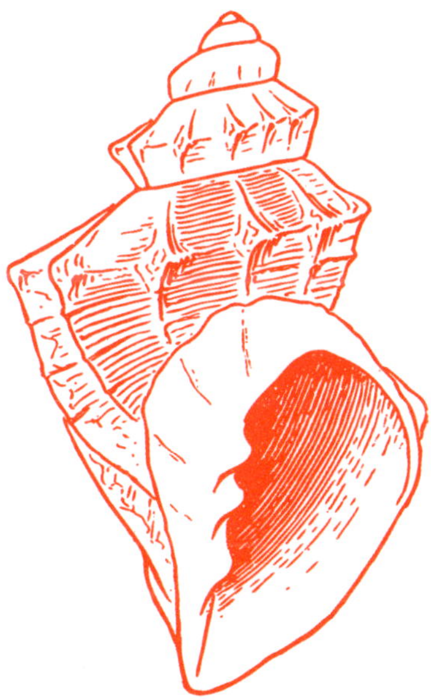

Of His Divine Poems

When we for Age could neither read nor write,
The subject made us able to indite;
The Soul, with nobler Resolutions deckt,
The Body stooping, does Herself erect:
No Mortal Parts, are requisite to raise
Her, that Unbodied can her Maker praise.
    The seas are quiet, when the Winds give o'er;
So calm are we, when Passions are no more:
For then we know how vain it is to boast
Of fleeting Things, so certain to be lost.
Clouds of Affection from our younger Eyes
Conceal that emptiness, which Age descries.
    The Soul's dark Cottage, batter'd and decay'd,
Lets in new Light, thro' chinks that time has made;
Stronger by weakness, wiser men become
As they draw near to their Eternal home.
Leaving the old, both Worlds at once they view,
That stand upon the threshold of the New.

by Edmund Waller

Yet a Little Sleep

Beside the drowsy streams that creep
Within this island of repose,
Oh, let us rest from cares and woes,
Oh, let us fold our hands to sleep!

Is it ignoble, then, to keep
Awhile from where the rough wind blows,
And all is strife, and no man knows
What end awaits him on the deep?

The voyager may rest awhile,
When rest invites, and yet may be
Neither a sluggard nor a craven.
With strength renewed he quits the isle,
And putting out again to sea,
Makes sail for his desired haven.

by Robert Fuller Murray

Shadows

And if tonight my soul may find her peace
in sleep, and sink in good oblivion,
and in the morning wake like a new-opened flower
then I have been dipped again in God, and new-created.

And if, as weeks go round, in the dark of the moon
my spirit darkens and goes out, and soft, strange gloom
pervades my movements and my thoughts and words
then I shall know that I am walking still
with God, we are close together now the moon's in shadow.

And if, as autumn deepens and darkens
I feel the pain of falling leaves, and stems that break in storms
and trouble and dissolution and distress
and then the softness of deep shadows folding, folding
around my soul and spirit, around my lips
so sweet, like a swoon, or more like the drowse of a low, sad song
singing darker than the nightingale, on, on to the solstice
and the silence of short days, the silence of the year, the shadow,
then I shall know that my life is moving still
with the dark earth, and drenched
with the deep oblivion of earth's lapse and renewal.

And if, in the changing phases of man's life
I fall in sickness and in misery
my wrists seem broken and my heart seems dead
and strength is gone, and my life
is only the leavings of a life:

and still, among it all, snatches of lovely oblivion,
  and snatches of renewal
odd, wintry flowers upon the withered stem, yet new,
strange flowers such as my life has not brought forth before,
new blossoms of me –

then I must know that still
I am in the hands of the unknown God,
he is breaking me down to his own oblivion
to send me forth on a new morning, a new man.

by D. H. Lawrence

To Hope

When by my solitary hearth I sit,
When no fair dreams before my - mind's eye - flit,
And the bare heath of life presents no bloom;
Sweet Hope, ethereal balm upon me shed,
And wave thy silver pinions o'er my head.

Whene'er I wander, at the fall of night,
Where woven boughs shut out the moon's bright ray,
Should sad Despondency my musings fright,
And frown, to drive fair Cheerfulness away,
Peep with the moon-beams through the leafy roof,
And keep that fiend Despondence far aloof.

Should Disappointment, parent of Despair,
Strive for her son to seize my careless heart;
When, like a cloud, he sits upon the air,
Preparing on his spell-bound prey to dart:
Chase him away, sweet Hope, with visage bright,
And fright him as the morning frightens night!

Whene'er the fate of those I hold most dear
Tells to my fearful breast a tale of sorrow,
O bright-eyed Hope, my morbid fancy cheer;
Let me awhile thy sweetest comforts borrow:
Thy heaven-born radiance around me shed,
And wave thy silver pinions o'er my head!

Should e'er unhappy love my bosom pain,
From cruel parents, or relentless fair;
O let me think it is not quite in vain
To sigh out sonnets to the midnight air!
Sweet Hope, ethereal balm upon me shed,
And wave thy silver pinions o'er my head!

In the long vista of the years to roll,
Let me not see our country's honour fade:
O let me see our land retain her soul,
Her pride, her freedom; and not freedom's shade.
From thy bright eyes unusual brightness shed -
Beneath thy pinions canopy my head!

Let me not see the patriot's high bequest,
Great Liberty! how great in plain attire!
With the base purple of a court oppress'd,
Bowing her head, and ready to expire:
But let me see thee stoop from heaven on wings
That fill the skies with silver glitterings!

And as, in sparkling majesty, a star
Gilds the bright summit of some gloomy cloud;
Brightening the half veil'd face of heaven afar:
So, when dark thoughts my boding spirit shroud,
Sweet Hope, celestial influence round me shed,
Waving thy silver pinions o'er my head.

by John Keats

And So To Bed

To rise with gratitude, to find one's destined sphere,
to feel that work is good, and hold it dear;
to take life's winding road with laughter and with song,
nor grumble at the load, though way be long ...
To pluck a harmful weed and plant a blossom there,
to see another's need, his burdens share;
to laugh, and joke a bit, to cherish one true friend,
preserve a gentle wit unto the end ...
To find in little things one's greatest happiness,
the bird that sweetly sings, the wind's caress;
to reach the Inn of Rest, and know the day has sped;
to breathe, 'I've done my best' – and so to bed.

by Wilhelmina Stitch

On a Quiet Conscience

Close thine eyes, and sleep secure:

They soul is safe, thy body pure.

He that guards thee, He that keeps,

Never slumbers, never sleeps.

A quiet conscience, in a quiet breast

Has only peace, has only rest:

The wisest and the mirth of kings

Are out of tune unless she sings.

Then close thine eyes in peace, and sleep secure,

No sleep so sweet as thine, no rest so sure.

by Charles I, King of England, Scotland, and Ireland

The World

I wish this world and its green hills were mine,
But it is not; the wandering shepherd star
Is not more distant, gazing from afar
On the unreaped pastures of the sea,
Than I am from the world, the world from me.
At night the stars on milky way that shine
Seem things one might possess, but this round green
Is for the cows that rest, these and the sheep:
To them the slopes and pastures offer sleep;
My sleep I draw from the far fields of blue,
Whence cold winds come and go among the few
Bright stars we see and many more unseen.

Birds sing on earth all day among the flowers,
Taking no thought of any other thing
But their own hearts, for out of them they sing:
Their songs are kindred to the blossom heads,
Faint as the petals which the blackthorn sheds,
And like the earth – not alien songs as ours.
To them this greenness and this island peace
Are life and death and happiness in one;
Nor are they separate from the white sun,
Or those warm winds which nightly wash the deep
Or starlight in the valleys, or new sleep;
And from these things they ask for no release.

But we can never call this world our own,
Because we long for it, and yet we know
That should the great winds call us, we should go;
Should they come calling out across the cold,
We should rise up and leave the sheltered fold
And follow the great road to the unknown,
We should pass by the barns and haystacks brown,
Should leave the wild pool and the nightingale;
Across the ocean we should set a sail
And, coming to the world's pale brim, should fly
Out to the very middle of the sky,
On past the moon; nor should we once look down.

by Fredegond Shove

May the Road Rise Up to Meet You

May the road rise up to meet you.
May the wind be always at your back.
May the sun shine warm upon your face;
the rains fall soft upon your fields
and until we meet again,
may God hold you in the palm of His hand.

by Anon. (traditional Gaelic blessing)

O To Be Up and Doing

O to be up and doing,
Unfearing and unashamed to go
In all the uproar and the press
About my human business!
My undissuaded heart I hear
Whisper courage in my ear.
With voiceless calls, the ancient earth
Summons me to a daily birth,
Thou, O my love, ye, O my friends –
The gist of life, the end of ends –
To laugh, to love, to live, to die
Ye call me by the ear and eye!

by Robert Louis Stevenson

Climbing

High up in the apple tree climbing I go,
With the sky above me, the earth below.
Each branch is the step of a wonderful stair
Which leads to the town I see shining up there.

Climbing, climbing, higher and higher,
The branches blow and I see a spire,
The gleam of a turret, the glint of a dome,
All sparkling and bright, like white sea foam.

On and on, from bough to bough,
The leaves are thick, but I push my way through;
Before, I have always had to stop,
But to-day I am sure I shall reach the top.

Today to the end of the marvelous stair,
Where those glittering pinacles flash in the air!
Climbing, climbing, higher I go,
With the sky close above me, the earth far below.

by Amy Lowell

Arbor Vitae *(extract)*

With honeysuckle, over-sweet, festoon'd;
With bitter ivy bound;
Terraced with funguses unsound;
Deform'd with many a boss
And closed scar, o'ercushion'd deep with moss;
Bunch'd all about with pagan mistletoe;
And thick with nests of the hoarse bird
That talks, but understands not his own word;
Stands, and so stood a thousand years ago,
A single tree.
Thunder has done its worst among its twigs,
Where the great crest yet blackens, never pruned,
But in its heart, alway
Ready to push new verdurous boughs, whene'er
The rotting saplings near it fall and leave it air,
Is all antiquity and no decay.
Rich, though rejected by the forest-pigs,
Its fruit, beneath whose rough, concealing rind
They that will break it find
Heat-succouring savour of each several meat,
And kernell'd drink of brain-renewing power,
With bitter condiment and sour,
And sweet economy of sweet,
And odours that remind
Of haunts of childhood and a different day.

by Coventry Patmore

Song of the Open Road *(extract)*

I

Afoot and light-hearted I take to the open road,
Healthy, free, the world before me,
The long brown path before me leading wherever I choose.

Henceforth I ask not good-fortune, I myself am good-fortune,
Henceforth I whimper no more, postpone no more, need nothing,
Done with indoor complaints, libraries, querulous criticisms,
Strong and content I travel the open road.

by Walt Whitman

Up-Hill

'Does the road wind up-hill all the way?'
    'Yes, to the very end.'
'Will the day's journey take the whole long day?'
    'From morn to night, my friend.'

'But is there for the night a resting-place?'
    'A roof for when the slow dark hours begin.'
'May not the darkness hide it from my face?'
    'You cannot miss that inn.'

'Shall I meet other wayfarers at night?'
    'Those who have gone before.'
'Then must I knock, or call when just in sight?'
    'They will not keep you standing at that door.'

'Shall I find comfort, travel-sore and weak?'
    'Of labour you shall find the sum.'
'Will there be beds for me and all who seek?'
    'Yea, beds for all who come.'

by Christina Rossetti

Diminishing Evils

How high those hills, how far away.
Menacing hills at break of day.
Friend, keep going; there's no knowing
when you will come to the end of the way.
Be not alarmed, fear not at all;
at the foot of the slope the hill looks small.
Journey along, hearty and strong,
the summit is reached e'er the shadows fall.
How great those ills, grim foes they seem.
Swift and swollen life's angry stream.
Friend, keep going, there's no knowing
when troubles will vanish as if in a dream.
Be not alarmed, have no fear;
the further away the worse they appear.
Journey along, hearty and strong;
troubles are bubbles when Courage is near.

by Wilhelmina Stitch

Life

Let me but live my life from year to year,
    With forward face and unreluctant soul;
    Not hurrying to, nor turning from, the goal;
Not mourning for the things that disappear
In the dim past, nor holding back in fear
    From what the future veils; but with a whole
    And happy heart, that pays its toll
To Youth and Age, and travels on with cheer.

So let the way wind up the hill or down,
    O'er rough or smooth, the journey will be joy:
    Still seeking what I sought when but a boy,
New friendship, high adventure, and a crown,
My heart will keep the courage of the quest,
And hope the road's last turn will be the best.

by Henry Van Dyke

Where Lies the Land?

Where lies the land to which the ship would go?
Far, far ahead, is all her seamen know.
And where the land she travels from? Away,
Far, far behind, is all that they can say.

On sunny noons upon the deck's smooth face,
Linked arm in arm, how pleasant here to pace;
Or, o'er the stern reclining, watch below
The foaming wake far widening as we go.

On stormy nights when wild north-westers rave,
How proud a thing to fight with wind and wave!
The dripping sailor on the reeling mast
Exults to bear, and scorns to wish it past.

Where lies the land to which the ship would go?
Far, far ahead, is all her seamen know.
And where the land she travels from? Away,
Far, far behind, is all that they can say.

by Arthur Hugh Clough

His Steady Sails He Never Furls

His steady sails he never furls
At any time o' year,
And perching now on Winter's curls,
He whistles in his ear

by Henry David Thoreau

Recognition

The old volcanic mountains
That slope up from the sea—
They dream and dream a thousand years
And watch what-is-to-be.

What gladness shines upon them
When, white as white sea-foam,
To the old, old ports of Beauty
A new sail comes home!

by Willa Cather

There is a Strength

There is a strength in proving that it can be borne
Although it tear –
What are the sinews of such cordage for
Except to bear
The ship might be of satin had it not to fight –
To walk on seas requires cedar Feet

by Emily Dickinson

Magna est Veritas

Here, in this little Bay,
Full of tumultuous life and great repose,
Where, twice a day,
The purposeless, glad ocean comes and goes,
Under high cliffs, and far from the huge town,
I sit me down.
For want of me the world's course will not fail:
When all its work is done, the lie shall rot;
The truth is great, and shall prevail,
When none cares whether it prevail or not.

by Coventry Patmore

Elegiac Stanzas Suggested by a Picture of Peele Castle in a Storm, Painted by Sir George Beaumont *(extract)*

O 'tis a passionate Work! – yet wise and well,
Well chosen is the spirit that is here;
That hulk which labours in the deadly swell,
This rueful sky, this pageantry of fear!

And this huge Castle, standing here sublime,
I love to see the look with which it braves,
Cased in the lightning armour of old Time,
The lightning, the fierce wind, and trampling waves.

Farewell, farewell the heart that lives alone,
Housed in a dream, at distance from the Kind!
Such happiness, wherever it be known,
Is to be pitied, for 'tis surely blind.

But welcome fortitude and patient cheer,
And frequent sights of what is to be borne!
Such sights, or worse, as are before me here, –
Not without hope we suffer and we mourn.

by William Wordsworth

Seaweed

Sea-weed sways and sways and swirls

as if swaying were its form of stillness;

and if it flushes against fierce **rock**

it slips over it as shadows do, without hurting itself.

by D. H. Lawrence

Sonnet 318: On His Blindness

When I consider how my light is spent
E're half my days, in this dark world and wide,
And that one Talent which is death to hide,
Lodg'd with me useless, though my Soul more bent
To serve therewith my Maker, and present
My true account, lest he returning chide,
Doth God exact day-labour, light deny'd,
I fondly ask; But patience to prevent
That murmur, soon replies, God doth not need
Either man's work or his own gifts, who best
Bear his milde yoak, they serve him best, his State
Is Kingly. Thousands at his bidding speed
And post o'er Land and Ocean without rest:
They also serve who only stand and waite.

by John Milton

Don't Quit

When things go wrong as they sometimes will,
When the road you're trudging seems all uphill,
When the funds are low and the debts are high
And you want to smile, but you have to sigh,
When care is pressing you down a bit,
Rest, if you must, but don't you quit.

Life is queer with its twists and turns,
As every one of us sometimes learns,
And many a failure turns about
When he might have won had he stuck it out,
Don't give up though the pace seems slow –
You may succeed with another blow.

Success is failure turned inside out –
The silver tint of the clouds of doubt,
And you never can tell how close you are,
It may be near when it seems so far,
So stick to the fight when you're hardest hit –
It's when things seem worst that you must not quit.

For all the sad words of tongue or pen,
The saddest are these: 'It might have been!'

by John Greenleaf Whittier

A Noiseless Patient Spider

A
noiseless
patient spider,
I mark'd where on a little promontory it stood isolated,
Mark'd how to explore the vacant vast surrounding,

It launch'd forth filament, filament, filament,
out of itself,
Ever unreeling them, ever tirelessly speeding them.

And you O my soul where you stand,
Surrounded, detached, in measureless
oceans of space,
Ceaselessly musing, venturing,
throwing, seeking the spheres
to connect them,

Till the bridge you will need be form'd, till the ductile anchor hold,
Till the gossamer thread you fling
catch somewhere,
O my soul.

by Walt Whitman

Departed Youth

What though the rosebuds from my cheek
Have faded all! which once so sleek
Spoke youth, and joy, and careless thought.
By guilt, or fear, or shame uncaught,
My soul, uninjured, still hath youth,
Its lively sense attests the truth!
Oh! I can wander yet, and taste
The beauties of the flowery waste,
The nightingale's deep swell can feel
Till to the eye a tear doth steal;
Rapt! gaze upon the gem-decked night,
Or mark the clear moon's gradual flight,
Whilst the bright river's rippled wave
Repeats the quivering beams she gave.
Nor yet does Painting strive in vain
To waken from its canvas plain
The lofty passions of the mind,
Or hint the sentiment refined:
To the sweet magic yet I bow,
As when youth decked my polished brow.
The chisel's lightest touch to trace
Through the pure form, or softened grace,
Is lent me still; I still admire,
And kindle at the Poet's fire—

Why Time! since these are left me still,
Of lesser thefts e'en take thy fill.
Yes, take all lustre from my eye,
And let the blithe carnation fly,
My tresses sprinkle o'er with snow,
That boasted once their auburn glow,
Break the slim form that was adored
By him so loved, my wedded lord;
But leave me, whilst all these you steal,
The mind to taste, the nerve to feel!

by Hannah Cowley

Life, the Teacher

Here is a truth the years have slowly taught me.
There's not an effort ever made in vain;
though fate within its painful clutch has caught me,
farther along the road I've gone—through pain.

Here is a lesson life has slowly taught me:
to chase good Fortune is young folly's way.
Always I've found that she herself has sought me
when love of work alone has filled my day.

There's not a fault that I have e'er committed,
there's no mistake that I have ever made,
that has not into life's mosaic fitted;
this is a law that is ever obeyed.

There's not a thread I've used, though it be knotted,
but has in my life's pattern found its place.
There's not a page, though with mistakes it's blotted,
that does not show of destiny some trace.

Here is a truth that I have grown to cherish:
no righteous battle's ever fought in vain;
nor does a thought or deed of goodness perish,
but, like a tree, brings forth its fruit again.

by Wilhelmina Stitch

To the Generation Knocking at the Door

Break — break it open; let the knocker rust:
Consider no 'Shalt not,' nor no man's 'must';
And, being entered, promptly take the lead,
Setting aside tradition, custom, creed;
Nor watch the balance of the huckster's beam;
Declare your hardiest thought, your proudest dream;
Await no summons; laugh at all rebuff;
High hearts and youth are destiny enough.
The mystery and the power enshrined in you
Are old as time and as the moment new:
And none but you can tell what part you play,
Nor can you tell until you make assay,
For this alone, this always, will succeed,
The miracle and magic of the deed.

by John Davidson

It is Everywhere

Green leaves. Wind kissed.
Closed palms. Fresh hope.

Deep river. Free flow.
No signs. Open road.

Wide sky. Grow wings.
Feel light. Dream big.

No frame. New eyes.
From dark. Find light.

Hug air. Laugh loud.
Breathe deep. Dance wild.

Smile wide. Shut eyes.
Hold chest. Close mind.

Ask cloud. Ask wind.
Ask earth. Ask field.

How to live free?

Hold on. Let Go.
Give trust. Lend heart.

Fall down. Get up.
Eat fear. Drink hope.

by Remi Graves

Courage

O heart, hold thee secure
In this blind hour of stress,
Live on, love on, endure,
Uncowed, though comfortless.

Life's still the wondrous thing
It seemed in bygone peace,
Though woe now jar the string,
And all its music cease.

Even if thine own self have
No haven for defence;
Stand not the unshaken brave
To give thee confidence?

Worse than all worst 'twould be,
If thou, who art thine all,
Shatter ev'n their reality
    In thy poor fall!

by Walter de la Mare

The Rainy Day

The day is cold, and dark, and dreary;
It rains, and the wind is never weary;
The vine still clings to the mouldering wall,
But at every gust the dead leaves fall,
    And the day is dark and dreary.

My life is cold, and dark, and dreary;
It rains, and the wind is never weary;
My thoughts still cling to the mouldering Past,
But the hopes of youth fall thick in the blast,
    And the days are dark and dreary.

Be still, sad heart! and cease repining;
Behind the clouds is the sun still shining;
Thy fate is the common fate of all,
Into each life some rain must fall,
    Some days must be dark and dreary.

by Henry Wadsworth Longfellow

If All Were Rain and Never Sun

If all were *rain* and never *sun*,

No bow could SPAN the *hill*;

If all were *sun* and never *rain*,

There'd be no *rainbow* still.

by Christina Rossetti

Hope

'Tis borne on the zephyr at eventide's hour;
It falls on the heart like the dew on the flower,–
An infinite essence from tropic to pole,
The promise, the home, and the heaven of Soul.

Hope happifies life, at the altar or bower,
And loosens the fetters of pride and of power;
It comes through our tears, as the soft summer rain,
To beautify, bless, and make joyful again.

The harp of the minstrel, the treasure of time;
A rainbow of rapture, o'erarching, divine;
The God-given mandate that speaks from above,–
No place for earth's idols, but hope thou, and love.

by Mary Baker Eddy

Joy and Sorrow

Then a woman said, Speak to us of Joy and Sorrow.
And he answered:
Your joy is your sorrow unmasked.
And the selfsame well from which your laughter rises
was oftentimes filled with your tears.
And how else can it be?
The deeper that sorrow carves into your being, the more
joy you can contain.
Is not the cup that holds your wine the very cup that was
burned in the potter's oven?
And is not the lute that soothes your spirit, the very wood that was
hollowed with knives?
When you are joyous, look deep into your heart and you shall find it
is only that which has given you sorrow that is giving you joy.
When you are sorrowful look again in your heart, and you shall see
that in truth you are weeping for that which has been your delight.

Some of you say, "Joy is greater than sorrow," and others say,
"Nay, sorrow is the greater."
But I say unto you, they are inseparable.
Together they come, and when one sits alone with you at your
board, remember that the other is asleep upon your bed.

Verily you are suspended like scales between your sorrow
and your joy.
Only when you are empty are you at standstill and balanced.
When the treasure-keeper lifts you to weigh his gold and
his silver, needs must your joy or your sorrow rise or fall.

by Kahlil Gibran

Auguries of Innocence *(extract)*

It is right it should be so
Man was made for Joy & Woe
And when this we rightly know
Thro the World we safely go
Joy & Woe are woven fine
A Clothing for the soul divine
Under every grief & pine
Runs a joy with silken twine.

by William Blake

Epigram

My soul, sit thou a patient looker-on;
Judge not the play before the play is done:
Her plot has many changes; every day
Speaks a new scene; the last act crowns the play.

by Frances Quarles

Life

Life, *believe*, is not a dream
So **DARK** as sages say;
Oft a little morning rain
Foretells a *pleasant* day.
Sometimes there are clouds of **gloom**,
But these are transient all;
If the shower will make the roses ***bloom***,
O why lament its *fall*?
Rapidly, merrily,
Life's sunny hours flit by,
Gratefully, cheerily
Enjoy them as they fly!
What though **DEATH** at times steps in,
And calls our Best away?
What though sorrow seems to win,
O'er hope, a **heavy sway?**
Yet Hope again elastic springs,
Unconquered, though *she fell*;

Still buoyant are her golden wings,
Still strong to bear us well.
Manfully, fearlessly,
The day of trial bear,
For gloriously, victoriously,
Can **COURAGE** quell **DESPAIR!**

by Charlotte Brontë

Solitude

Laugh, and the world laughs with you;
Weep, and you weep alone;
For the sad old earth must borrow its mirth,
But has trouble enough of its own.
Sing, and the hills will answer;
Sigh, it is lost on the air;
The echoes bound to a joyful sound,
But shrink from voicing care.

Rejoice, and men will seek you;
Grieve, and they turn and go;
They want full measure of all your pleasure,
But they do not need your woe.
Be glad, and your friends are many;
Be sad, and you lose them all,—
There are none to decline your nectared wine,
But alone you must drink life's gall.

Feast, and your halls are crowded;
Fast, and the world goes by.
Succeed and give, and it helps you live,
But no man can help you die.
There is room in the halls of pleasure
For a large and lordly train,
But one by one we must all file on
Through the narrow aisles of pain.

by Ella Wheeler Wilcox

The Lake of Gaube *(extract)*

Whose thought has fathomed and measured
The darkness of life and of death,
The secret within them treasured,
The spirit that is not breath?
Whose vision has yet beholden
The splendor of death and of life?
Though sunset as dawn be golden,
Is the word of them peace, not strife?
Deep silence answers: the glory
We dream of may be but a dream,
And the sun of the soul wax hoary
As ashes that show not a gleam.
But well shall it be with us ever
Who drive through the darkness here,
If the soul that we live by never,
For aught that a lie saith, fear.

by Algernon Charles Swinburne

Give Me Strength *(extract)*

GIVE ME THE
STRENGTH
lightly to bear my joys and sorrows.

GIVE ME THE
STRENGTH
to make my love fruitful in service.

GIVE ME THE
STRENGTH
never to disown the poor or bend my
knees before insolent might.

GIVE ME THE
STRENGTH
to raise my mind high above daily trifles.

AND GIVE ME THE
STRENGTH
to surrender my strength to thy will
with love.

by Rabindranath Tagore

Strength

Be strong to hope, O heart!
    Though day is bright,
The stars can only shine
    In the dark night.
Be strong, O heart of mine,
    Look toward the light.

Be strong to bear, O heart!
    Nothing is vain:
Strive not, for life is care,
    And God sends pain.
Heaven is above, and there
    Rest will remain.

Be strong to love, O heart!
    Love knows not wrong;
Didst thou love creatures even,
    Life were not long;
Didst thou love God in heaven
    Thou wouldst be strong.

Why comes temptation but for man to meet
And master and make crouch beneath his foot,
And so be pedestaled in triumph? Pray,
"Lead us into no such temptation, Lord!"
Yea, but, O thou whose servants are the bold,
Lead such temptations by the head and hair,
Reluctant dragons, up to who dares fight,
That so he may do battle and have praise.

by Robert Browning

Endure Hardness

A cold wind stirs the blackthorn
    To burgeon and to blow,
Besprinkling half-green hedges
    With flakes and sprays of snow.

Through coldness and through keenness,
    Dear hearts, take comfort so:
Somewhere or other doubtless
    These make the blackthorn blow.

by Christina Rossetti

In Our Time

Between the rough hills of gabbro and the cold sea,
Between the factory hooter and the snub-nosed bullet,
Folly grows up to its full height, but cannot grow for ever.

Folly is built on pride, on pride and power,
And power ends in weariness and duty:
Even the hooded eagle cannot soar to heaven.

And the leader looks at last toward the people,
People asking for a home, a plot of earth,
A pageant in spring, and a sight of foreign merchants.

Power is built on fear and empty bellies:
Between the rough hills of gabbro and the cold sea
The gulls scream, squabbling for a poor harvest.

Between the factory hooter and the snub-nosed bullet,
Under the shadow of the guns, the corn ripens,
And folly cannot die, but cannot grow for ever.

by Michael Roberts

The Waterfall *(extract)*

With what deep murmurs through time's silent stealth
Doth thy transparent, cool, and watery wealth

Here flowing fall,
And chide and call,

As if his liquid loose retinue stayed
Lingering, and were of this steep place afraid,

The common pass
Where, clear as glass,
All must descend
Not to an end;

But quickened by this deep and rocky grave,
Rise to a longer course more bright and brave.

by Henry Vaughn

Demogorgon's Speech

This is the day, which down the void abysm
At the Earth-born's spell yawns for Heaven's despotism,
    And Conquest is dragged captive through the deep:
Love, from its awful throne of patient power
In the wise heart, from the last giddy hour
    Of dread endurance, from the slippery, steep,
And narrow verge of crag-like agony, springs
And folds over the world its healing wings.

Gentleness, Virtue, Wisdom and Endurance,
These are the seals of that most firm assurance
    Which bars the pit over Destruction's strength;
And if, with infirm hand, Eternity,
Mother of many acts and hours, should free
    The serpent that would clasp her with his length;
These are the spells by which to reassume
An empire o'er the disentangled doom.

To suffer woes which Hope thinks infinite;
To forgive wrongs darker than death or night;
    To defy Power, which seems omnipotent;
To love, and bear; to hope till Hope creates
From its own wreck the thing it contemplates;
    Neither to change, nor falter, nor repent;
This, like thy glory, Titan, is to be
Good, great and joyous, beautiful and free;
This is alone Life, Joy, Empire, and Victory.

by Percy Bysshe Shelley

Belief

Forever *nameless*
Forever *unknown*
Forever *unconceived*
Forever *unrepresented*
yet forever felt in the *soul.*

by D. H. Lawrence

I Shall Return

I shall return again; I shall return
To laugh and love and watch with wonder-eyes
At golden noon the forest fires burn,
Wafting their blue-black smoke to sapphire skies.
I shall return to loiter by the streams
That bathe the brown blades of the bending grasses,
And realize once more my thousand dreams
Of waters rushing down the mountain passes.
I shall return to hear the fiddle and fife
Of village dances, dear delicious tunes
That stir the hidden depths of native life,
Stray melodies of dim remembered runes.
I shall return, I shall return again,
To ease my mind of long, long years of pain.

by Claude McKay

A Refusal

Sith Fortune favours not,
  and all things backward go,
And sith your mind hath so decreed
  to make an end of woe;
Sith now is no redress,
  but hence I must away –
Farewell – I waste no vainer words,
  I hope for better day.

by Barnabe Googe

What Are Heavy?

WHAT ARE HEAVY?
Sea-sand and sorrow:

WHAT ARE BRIEF?
To-day and to-morrow:

WHAT ARE FRAIL?
Spring blossoms and youth:

WHAT ARE DEEP?
The ocean and truth.

by Christina Rossetti

Let No Charitable Hope

Now let no charitable hope
Confuse my mind with images
Of eagle and of antelope:
I am in nature none of these.

I was, being human, born alone;
I am, being woman, hard beset;
I live by squeezing from a stone
The little nourishment I get.

In masks outrageous and austere
The years go by in single file;
But none has merited my fear,
And none has quite escaped my smile.

by Elinor Wylie

Riches I Hold in Light Esteem

Riches I hold in light esteem
And Love I laugh to scorn
And lust of Fame was but a dream
That vanished with the morn –

And if I pray – the only prayer
That moves my lips for me
Is – 'Leave the heart that now I bear
And give me liberty.'

Yes, as my swift days near their goal:
'Tis all that I implore –
Through life and death, a chainless soul
With courage to endure!

by Emily Brontë

The Songs I Had

The songs I had are withered
Or vanished clean,
Yet there are bright tracks
Where I have been,

And there grow flowers
For other's delight.
Think well, O singer,
Soon comes night.

by Ivor Gurney

A Vision

I lost the love of heaven *above*
I spurned the lust of earth *below*
I felt the sweets of fancied *love*
And hell itself my only *foe*

I lost earth's joys but felt the *glow*
Of heaven's flame abound in *me*
Till loveliness and I did *grow*
The bard of *immortality*

I loved but woman fell *away*
I hid me from her faded *fame*
I snatched the sun's eternal *ray*
And wrote till earth was but a *name*

In every language upon *earth*
On every shore, o'er every *sea*,
I give my name immortal *birth*,
And kept my spirit with the *free*

by John Clare

Epitaph

Life is a jest; and all things show it,
I thought so once; but now I know it.

by John Gay

If I Can Stop One Heart from Breaking

If I can stop one heart from breaking
I shall not live in vain;
If I can ease one life the aching,
Or cool one pain,
Or help one fainting robin
Unto his nest again,
I shall not live in vain.

by Emily Dickinson

CHAPTER TWO

You Are Not Alone

"I lift my lamp beside the golden door!"

The New Colossus, Emma Lazarus

The Celestial Announcer

On the day that you hear
the station announcer
call out the towns and villages
of your life, as if she'd read
the very chapters of your soul,
that knowing way she has of saying *Halifax*,
the way she skirts around poor rainy *Manchester*,
and jumps to the conclusion now of *Luddenden*
– with its ghost of a station
and dream of Branwell drunk under the stars –
and all the big and little places
you have ever been, would like to go,
chanted, charted;
well, then you realise it's time to change
your mind, ticket, journey,
point of departure,
Estimated Time of Arrival
and know that she will lend you wings
for those golden slippers, milk and honey,
bread, roses and a brand new map.

by Maura Dooley

The New Colossus

Not like the brazen giant of Greek fame,
With conquering limbs astride from land to land;
Here at our sea-washed, sunset gates shall stand
A mighty woman with a torch, whose flame
Is the imprisoned lightning, and her name
Mother of Exiles. From her beacon-hand
Glows world-wide welcome; her mild eyes command
The air-bridged harbor that twin cities frame.
"Keep, ancient lands, your storied pomp!" cries she
With silent lips. "Give me your tired, your poor,
Your huddled masses yearning to breathe free,
The wretched refuse of your teeming shore.
Send these, the homeless, tempest-tost to me,
I lift my lamp beside the golden door!"

by Emma Lazarus

Santa Filomena

Whene'er a noble deed is wrought,
Whene'er is spoken a noble thought,
  Our hearts, in glad surprise,
  To higher levels rise.

The tidal wave of deeper souls
Into our inmost being rolls,
  And lifts us unawares
  Out of all meaner cares.

Honor to those whose words or deeds
Thus help us in our daily needs,
  And by their overflow
  Raise us from what is low!

Thus thought I, as by night I read
Of the great army of the dead,
  The trenches cold and damp,
  The starved and frozen camp, –

The wounded from the battle-plain,
In dreary hospitals of pain,
  The cheerless corridors,
  The cold and stony floors.

Lo! in that house of misery
A lady with a lamp I see
  Pass through the glimmering gloom,
  And flit from room to room.

And slow, as in a dream of bliss,
The speechless sufferer turns to kiss
    Her shadow, as it falls
    Upon the darkening walls.

As if a door in heaven should be
Opened, and then closed suddenly,
    The vision came and went,
    The light shone was spent.

On England's annals, through the long
Hereafter of her speech and song,
    That light its rays shall cast
    From portals of the past.

A Lady with a Lamp shall stand
In the great history of the land,
    A noble type of good,
    Heroic womanhood.

Nor even shall be wanting here
The palm, the lily, and the spear,
    The symbols that of yore
    Saint Filomena bore.

by Henry Wadsworth Longfellow

Libraries Exist

Libraries exist, i repeat like a prayer between lips
walking streets, reading news about hate
they didn't always exist, libraries
these spaces of open-armed refuge, until one day,
perhaps in the heat of a summer,
or whilst trudging through snow, somewhere
a man or a woman or both, seeing children or adults
desperate for stories and warmth,
and the idea was born, and it spread, it spread,
like seedlings sprout between rubble,
like peace between gunshot, heat between hugs
until country upon country, village upon village
in a building, or a bus between houses
in a school or a phone booth abandoned,
books, lined up like offerings for no reason other than love
libraries exist, i repeat to myself, when the news
brings us nothing but profit and bloodshed,
when faith in humanity seems a distant horizon:
once upon a time there were none in the world, libraries,
and now somewhere in the struggle
between hatred and hope,
a child is choosing a book to take home,
believing they are worth every word

by Hollie McNish

Heartbreak Road

As I went up by Heartbreak Road
    Before the dawn of day,
The cold mist was all about,
    And the wet world was gray;
It seemed that never another soul
    Had walked that weary way.

But when I came to Heartbreak Hill,
    Silver touched the sea;
I knew that many and many a soul
    Was climbing close to me;
I knew I walked that weary way
    In a great company.

by Helen Gray Cone

Fellowship

I

In the old accents I will sing, my Glory, my Delight,
In the old accents, tipped with flame, before we knew the right,
True way of singing with reserve. O Love, with pagan might,

II

White in our steeds, and white too in our armour let us ride,
Immortal, white, triumphing, flashing downward side by side
To where our friends, the Argonauts, are fighting with the tide.

III

Let us draw calm to them, Beloved, the souls on heavenly voyage bound,
Saluting as one presence. Great disaster were it found,
If one with half-fed lambency should halt and flicker round.

IV

O friends so fondly loving, so beloved, look up to us,
In constellation breaking on your errand, prosperous,
O Argonauts!

    Now, faded from their sight,
We cling and joy. It was thy intercession gave me right
My Fellow, to this fellowship. My Glory, my Delight!

by Michael Field (Katherine Bradley & Edith Cooper)

Travel

The railroad track is miles away,
    And the day is loud with voices speaking,
Yet there isn't a train goes by all day
    But I hear its whistle shrieking.

All night there isn't a train goes by,
    Though the night is still for sleep and dreaming,
But I see its cinders red on the sky,
    And hear its engine steaming.

My heart is warm with the friends I make,
    And better friends I'll not be knowing,
Yet there isn't a train I wouldn't take,
    No matter where it's going.

by Edna St Vincent Millay

Sonnet 30

When to the sessions of sweet silent thought
I summon up remembrance of things past,
I sigh the lack of many a thing I sought,
And with old woes new wail my dear time's waste;
Then can I drown an eye, unused to flow,
For precious friends hid in death's dateless night,
And weep afresh love's long since cancelled woe,
And moan th' expense of many a vanished sight;
Then can I grieve at grievances foregone,
And heavily from woe to woe tell o'er
The sad account of fore-bemoanèd moan,
Which I new pay as if not paid before.
    But if the while I think on thee, dear friend,
    All losses are restored, and sorrows end.

by William Shakespeare

Time Flies

Time flies, Suns rise

And shadows fall.

Let time go by.

Love is **forever** over all.

by Anon. (found on an English sundial)

My Comforter

Well has thou spoken and yet not taught
A feeling strange or new –
Thou hast but roused a latent thought,
A cloud-closed beam of sunshine brought
To gleam in open view –

Deep down – concealed within my soul
That light lies hid from men
Yet glows unquenched though shadows roll,
Its gentle ray cannot control,
– About the sullen den –

Was I not vexed, in these gloomy ways
To walk unlit so long?
Around me, wretches uttering praise
Or howling o'er their hopeless days –
And each with frenzy's tongue –

A Brotherhood of misery,
With smiles as sad as sighs –
Whose madness daily maddening me,
Turning into agony
The Bliss before my eyes –

So stood I – in Heaven's glorious sun
And, in the glare of Hell
My spirit drank a mingled tone
Of seraph's song and demon's groan.
– What thy soul bore thy soul alone
Within its self may tell –

Like a soft air above a sea,
Tossed by the tempest's stir –
A thawwind, melting quietly
The snowdrift on some wintery lea
– No – What sweet thing can match with thee,
My thoughtful Comforter?

And yet a little longer speak
Calm this resentful mood
And while the savage heart grows meek,
For other token do not seek,
But let the tear upon my cheek
Evince my gratitude –

by Emily Brontë

Sonnet with Lighthouses

The first lighthouse is you.

The second lighthouse is you, age 12, turned around beneath a wave.

The third lighthouse is a hyperbaric chamber you clamber into when you dive too deep and rise too fast, an oil-dark depth that's child's play for trained divers but you, girl, you clawed yourself up –

The fourth lighthouse tunes into the shipping song over sea static: rain later, good, occasionally poor.

The fifth lighthouse says over and over, I love you I love you I love you you you you there.

Every wall in the sixth lighthouse is load-bearing.

The seventh lighthouse is a scattergram of light that indicates the strength and direction between two variables: ship and safe harbour, moon and tide, shore and vagaries of current, each of us to each other, our future selves to our past selves, every dear friend placed at strategic vantage points in our life.

Just seeing the eighth lighthouse strengthens your circuitry, blood zinging around your bones in delight.

The ninth lighthouse has *worse things happen at sea* cheerfully cross-stitched on a pillow it bought drunk off Etsy.

The tenth lighthouse sometimes just wants to be a lifeboat or a ladder or an oxygen mask, dropped down in case of emergencies and not always looking out for other people when they can't help themselves.

The eleventh lighthouse's favourite piece of furniture is the walnut drop-leaf table that opens so everyone can fit around it.

The twelfth lighthouse makes you feel like stepping out of time.

The thirteenth lighthouse comforts you with Fermat's mathematical proof which shows that light knows where it's going, that it takes the shortest possible route, even through water and gale forces.

The fourteenth lighthouse hollers MARCO.
POLO, everyone you love shouts back.

by Cynthia Miller

The Awakening

There is a veteran tree,
With green-stained bark,
Rising like a tower of the sea,
From the smooth park.
He is a giant among trees,
And he has watched this house for centuries.

His bark is hard as rock,
Time and Sun and the Wind's shock
Have twisted his boughs till they are like the
    arms of a great carven figure of Care,
Flung in passionate appeal to the changing
    humour of the Air.
Now on high branches sticky buds appear,
Promise of growth and beauty for the year.
It seems my life is an old tree,
And the young buds are your sweet love for me.

by Anna Wickham

Beauty That is Never Old

When buffeted and beaten by life's storms,
When by the bitter cares of life oppressed,
I want no surer haven than your arms,
I want no sweeter heaven than your breast.

When over my life's way there falls the blight
Of sunless days, and nights of starless skies;
Enough for me, the calm and steadfast light
That softly shines within your loving eyes.

The world, for me, and all the world can hold
Is circled by your arms; for me there lies,
Within the lights and shadows of your eyes,
The only beauty that is never old.

by James Weldon Johnson

A Chant Against Death

say *family*
say *friends*
say *wife*
say *love*
say *life*

say *learning*
laughter
sunlight
rain

say *cycle*
circle
music
memory

say *night* & *day*
say *sun* & *moon*

say
see you soon

by Mervyn Morris

New Year

In the coming year enfolded
    Bright and sad hours lie,
Waiting till you reach and live them
    As the year rolls by.

In the happy hours and radiant
    I would like to be
Somewhere out of sight, forgotten,
    Your delight to see.

But when you are tired and saddened,
    Vexed with life, dismayed,
I would steal your grief, and lay it
    Where my own is laid –

Bleed my heart out in your service
    If, set free from pain,
You, through me, found life worth living,
    Glad and fair again.

by Edith Nesbit

The Hut by the Sea

Here is my hut beside the hilly sea,
A sweet, small resting-place, so soft and warm,
Though framed by desolate immensity,
And rocked within the arms of every storm.

Each home where love abides is even so,
A steadfast joy beneath a changing sky;
And all the storms of life that round it blow
Are but its cradle and its lullaby.

by Ethelwyn Wetherald

Snow-Bound: A Winter Idyl *(extract)*

Shut in from all the world without
We sat the clean-winged hearth about,
Content to let the north-wind roar
In baffled rage at pane and door,
While the red logs before us beat
The frost-line back with tropic heat;
And ever, when a louder blast
Shook beam and rafter as it passed,
The merrier up its roaring draught
The great throat of the chimney laughed,
The house-dog on his paws outspread
Laid to the fire his drowsy head,
The cat's dark silhouette on the wall
A couchant tiger's seemed to fall;
And, for the winter fireside meet,
Between the andirons' straddling feet,
The mug of cider simmered slow,
The apples sputtered in a row,
And, close at hand, the basket stood
With nuts from brown October's wood.
What matter how the night behaved?
What matter how the north-wind raved?
Blow high, blow low, not all its snow
Could quench our hearth-fire's ruddy glow.

by John Greenleaf Whittier

The Consolation

Though bleak these woods, and damp the ground
With fallen leaves so thickly strown,
And cold the wind that wanders round
With wild and melancholy moan;

There *is* a friendly roof, I know,
Might shield me from the wintry blast;
There is a fire, whose ruddy glow
Will cheer me for my wanderings past.

And so, though still, where'er I go,
Cold stranger-glances meet my eye;
Though, when my spirit sinks in woe,
Unheeded swells the unbidden sigh;

Though solitude, endured too long,
Bids youthful joys too soon decay,
Makes mirth a stranger to my tongue,
And overclouds my noon of day;

When kindly thoughts that would have way,
Flow back discouraged to my breast; –
I know there *is*, though far away,
A home where heart and soul may rest.

Warm hands are there, that, clasped in mine,
The warmer heart will not belie;
While mirth, and truth, and friendship shine
In smiling lip and earnest eye.

The ice that gathers round my heart
May there be thawed; and sweetly, then,
The joys of youth, that now depart,
Will come to cheer my soul again.

Though far I roam, that thought shall be
My hope, my comfort, everywhere;
While such a home remains to me,
My heart shall never know despair!

by Anne Brontë

The Artist's Life: *Interpretation*

The dreamer found his house
Narrow and stained with years.
The wise man said 'How can this stand!
The tinder walls will fall,
The old roof crush that fool.'

But the garden of the house
Was full of kindly trees,
And brave birds built low nests on little shrubs,
And all small beasts were friends.
At night the marching stars stooped to the house,
And in blue brittle light Truth spoke.
A wanton and an old poor man
Strayed to the garden.
And in the charmed shadows, sang
A clear, clean song.
The dreamer laughed, 'Let the house fall!'

by Anna Wickham

A Song to David *(extract)*

Strong is the horse upon his speed;
Strong in pursuit the rapid glede,
    Which makes at once his game:
Strong the tall ostrich on the ground;
Strong through the turbulent profound
    Shoots xiphias to his aim.

Strong is the lion—like a coal
His eye-ball—like a bastion's mole
    His chest against the foes:
Strong, the gier-eagle on his sail,
Strong against tide, the enormous whale
    Emerges as he goes.

But stronger still, in earth and air,
And in the sea, the man of prayer;
    And far beneath the tide;
And in the seat to faith assigned,
Where ask is have, where seek is find,
    Where knock is open wide.

by Christopher Smart

Light Shining Out of Darkness

God moves in a mysterious way,
His wonders to perform;
He plants his footsteps in the sea,
And rides upon the storm.

Deep in unfathomable mines
Of never-failing skill,
He treasures up his bright designs,
And works his sovereign will.

Ye fearful saints, fresh courage take,
The clouds ye so much dread
Are big with mercy, and shall break
In blessings on your head.

Judge not the Lord by feeble sense,
But trust him for his grace;
Behind a frowning providence
He hides a smiling face.

His purposes will ripen fast,
Unfolding every hour;
The bud may have a bitter taste,
But sweet will be the flower.

Blind unbelief is sure to err,
And scan his work in vain:
God is his own interpreter,
And he will make it plain.

by William Cowper

The Shepherd Boy Sings in the Valley of Humiliation

He that is down needs fear no fall,
    He that is low, no pride;
He that is humble ever shall
    Have God to be his guide.

I am content with what I have,
    Little be it or much:
And, Lord, contentment still I crave,
    Because Thou savest such.

Fullness to such a burden is
    That go on pilgrimage:
Here little, and hereafter bliss,
    Is best from age to age.

by John Bunyan

No Coward Soul is Mine

No coward soul is mine,
No trembler in the world's storm-troubled sphere!
I see Heaven's glories shine,
And Faith shines equal, arming me from Fear.

O God within my breast,
Almighty, ever-present Deity!
Life, that in me hast rest,
As I, undying Life, have power in Thee!

Vain are the thousand creeds
That move men's hearts: unutterably vain;
Worthless as withered weeds,
Or idlest froth amid the boundless main,

To waken doubt in one
Holding so fast by thy infinity,
So surely anchored on
The steadfast rock of Immortality.

With wide-embracing love
Thy spirit animates eternal years,
Pervades and broods above,
Changes, sustains, dissolves, creates, and rears.

Though earth and moon were gone,
And suns and universes ceased to be,
And thou were left alone,
Every existence would exist in Thee.

There is not room for Death,
Nor atom that his might could render void:
Since thou art Being and Breath,
And what Thou art may never be destroyed.

by Emily Brontë

By the Statue of King Charles at Charing Cross *(extract)*

Yet, when the city sleeps;
When all the cries are still:
The stars and heavenly deeps
Work out a perfect will.

by Lionel Johnson

On the Sussex Downs

Over the downs there were birds flying,
    Far off glittered the sea,
And toward the north the weald of Sussex
    Lay like a kingdom under me.

I was happier than the larks
    That nest on the downs and sing to the sky –
Over the downs the birds flying
    Were not so happy as I.

It was not you, though you were near,
    Though you were good to hear and see,
It was not earth, it was not heaven,
    It was myself that sang in me.

by Sara Teasdale

CHAPTER THREE

Into Battle

"Marching fearless through the darkness"

L'Envoi
Emily Wilding Davison

Reveille

Wake: the silver dusk returning
    Up the beach of darkness brims,
And the ship of sunrise burning
    Strands upon the eastern rims.

Wake: the vaulted shadow shatters,
    Trampled to the floor it spanned,
And the tent of night in tatters
    Straws the sky-pavilioned land.

Up, lad, up, 'tis late for lying:
    Hear the drums of morning play;
Hark, the empty highways crying
    "Who'll beyond the hills away?"

Towns and countries woo together,
    Forelands beacon, belfries call;
Never lad that trod on leather
    Lived to feast his heart with all.

Up, lad: thews that lie and cumber
    Sunlit pallets never thrive;
Morns abed and daylight slumber
    Were not meant for man alive.

Clay lies still, but blood's a rover;
    Breath's a ware that will not keep.
Up, lad: when the journey's over
    There'll be time enough to sleep.

by A. E. Housman

On the Idle Hill of Summer

On the idle hill of summer,
Sleepy with the flow of streams,
Far I hear the steady drummer
Drumming like a noise in dreams.

Far and near and low and louder
On the roads of earth go by,
Dear to friends and food for powder,
Soldiers marching, all to die.

East and west on fields forgotten
Bleach the bones of comrades slain,
Lovely lads and dead and rotten;
None that go return again.

Far the calling bugles hollo,
High the screaming fife replies,
Gay the files of scarlet follow:
Woman bore me, I will rise.

by A.E. Housman

Heart of Oak *(extract)*

Come, cheer up, my lads, ’tis to glory we steer,
To add something more to this wonderful year.
To honour we call you, not press you like slaves,
For who are so free as we sons of the waves?

Chorus
Heart of oak are our ships, heart of oak are our men;
We always are ready—steady, boys, steady—
We’ll fight and we’ll conquer again and again.

by David Garrick

Henry VI, Part III, Act II, Scene I *(extract)*

EDWARD Dazzle mine eyes, or do I see three suns?

RICHARD Three glorious suns, each one a perfect sun;
Not separated with the racking clouds,
But severed in a pale clear-shining sky.
See, see! They join, embrace, and seem to kiss,
As if they vowed some league inviolable;
Now are they but one lamp, one light, one sun.
In this the heaven figures some event.

EDWARD 'Tis wondrous strange, the like yet never heard of.
I think it cites us, brother, to the field,
That we, the sons of brave Plantagenet,
Each one already blazing by our meeds,
Should notwithstanding join our lights together
And over-shine the earth, as this the world.
Whate'er it bodes, henceforward will I bear
Upon my target three fair-shining suns.

by William Shakespeare

The New Jerusalem

And did those feet in ancient time
Walk upon England's mountains green?
And was the holy Lamb of God
On England's pleasant pastures seen?

And did the Countenance Divine
Shine forth upon our clouded hills?
And was Jerusalem builded here
Among these dark Satanic Mills?

Bring me my Bow of burning gold:
Bring me my Arrows of desire:
Bring me my Spear: O clouds unfold!
Bring me my Chariot of fire.

I will not cease from Mental Fight,
Nor shall my Sword sleep in my hand
Till we have built Jerusalem
In England's green & pleasant Land.

by William Blake

The Wild Ride

I hear in my heart, I hear in its ominous pulses,
All day, on the road, the hoofs of invisible horses;
All night, from their stalls, the importunate tramping and neighing.

Let cowards and laggards fall back! but alert to the saddle,
Straight, grim, and abreast, go the weather-worn, galloping legion,
With a stirrup-cup each to the lily of women that loves him.

The trail is through dolor and dread, over crags and morasses;
There are shapes by the way, there are things that appal or entice us:
What odds? We are knights, and our souls are but bent on the riding.

I hear in my heart, I hear in its ominous pulses,
All day, on the road, the hoofs of invisible horses;
All night, from their stalls, the importunate tramping and neighing.

We spur to a land of no name, out-racing the storm-wind;
We leap to the infinite dark, like the sparks from the anvil.
Thou leadest, O God! All's well with Thy troopers that follow.

by Louise Imogen Guiney

The Charge of the Light Brigade

Half a league, half a league,
    Half a league onward,
All in the valley of Death
    Rode the six hundred.
'Forward, the Light Brigade!
Charge for the guns!' he said:
Into the valley of Death
    Rode the six hundred.

'Forward, the Light Brigade!'
Was there a man dismay'd?
    Not tho' the soldier knew
Some one had blunder'd:
Their's not to make reply,
Their's not to reason why,
Their's but to do and die:
Into the valley of Death
    Rode the six hundred.

Cannon to right of them,
Cannon to left of them,
Cannon in front of them
    Volley'd and thunder'd;
Storm'd at with shot and shell,
Boldly they rode and well,
Into the jaws of Death,
Into the mouth of Hell
    Rode the six hundred.

Flash'd all their sabres bare,
Flash'd as they turn'd in air
Sabring the gunners there,
Charging an army, while
    All the world wonder'd:
Plunged in the battery-smoke
Right thro' the line they broke;
Cossack and Russian
Reel'd from the sabre-stroke
    Shatter'd and sunder'd.
Then they rode back, but not
    Not the six hundred.

Cannon to right of them,
Cannon to left of them,
Cannon behind them
    Volley'd and thunder'd;
Storm'd at with shot and shell,
While horse and hero fell,
They that had fought so well
Came thro' the jaws of Death,
Back from the mouth of Hell,
All that was left of them,
    Left of six hundred.

When can their glory fade?
O the wild charge they made!
    All the world wonder'd.
Honour the charge they made!
Honour the Light Brigade,
    Noble six hundred!

by Alfred, Lord Tennyson

Casabianca

The boy stood on the burning deck,
Whence all but he had fled;
The flame that lit the battle's wreck
Shone round him o'er the dead.

Yet beautiful and bright he stood,
As born to rule the storm –
A creature of heroic blood,
A proud, though child-like form.

The flames rolled on – he would not go
Without his father's word;
That father, faint in death below,
His voice no longer heard.

He called aloud: – 'Say, Father, say,
If yet my task is done?'
He knew not that the chieftain lay
Unconscious of his son.

'Speak, Father!' once again he cried,
'If I may yet be gone!'
And but the booming shots replied,
And fast the flames rolled on.

Upon his brow he felt their breath,
And in his waving hair,
And looked from that lone post of death
In still yet brave despair;

And shouted but once more aloud,
'My Father! must I stay?'
While o'er him fast, through sail and shroud,
The wreathing fires made way.

They wrapt the ship in splendour wild,
They caught the flag on high,
And streamed above the gallant child,
Like banners in the sky.

There came a burst of thunder sound –
The boy – oh! where was he?
Ask of the winds that far around
With fragments strew'd the sea! –

With mast, and helm, and pennon fair,
That well had borne their part,
But the noblest thing that perished there
Was that young faithful heart!

by Felicia Dorothea Hemans

Full Moon at Tierz: Before the Storming of Huesca *(extract)*

The past, a glacier, gripped the mountain wall,
And time was inches, dark was all.
But here it scales the end of the range,
The dialectic's point of change,
Crashes in light and minutes to its fall.

Time present is a cataract whose force
Breaks down the banks even at its source
And history forming in our hands
Not plasticine but roaring sands,
Yet we must swing it to its final course.

The intersecting lines that cross both ways,
Time future, has no image in space,
Crooked as the road that we must tread,
Straight as our bullets fly ahead.
We are the future. The last fight let us face.

by John Cornford

Lepanto *(extract)*

Dim drums throbbing, in the hills half heard,
Where only on a nameless throne a crownless prince has stirred,
Where, risen from a doubtful seat and half attainted stall,
The last knight of Europe takes weapons from the wall,
The last and lingering troubadour to whom the bird has sung,
That once went singing southward when all the world was young,
In that enormous silence, tiny and unafraid,
Comes up along a winding road the noise of the Crusade.
Strong gongs groaning as the guns boom far,
Don John of Austria is going to the war,
Stiff flags straining in the night-blasts cold
In the gloom black-purple, in the glint old-gold,
Torchlight crimson on the copper kettle-drums,
Then the tuckets, then the trumpets, then the cannon, and he comes.
Don John laughing in the brave beard curled,
Spurning of his stirrups like the thrones of all the world,
Holding his head up for a flag of all the free.

by G. K. Chesterton

Epilogue to *Asolando*

At the midnight in the silence of the sleep-time,
    When you set your fancies free,
Will they pass to where – by death, fools think, imprisoned –
Low he lies who once so loved you, whom you loved so,
    – Pity me?

Oh to love so, be so loved, yet so mistaken!
What had I on earth to do
With the slothful, with the mawkish, the unmanly?
Like the aimless, helpless, hopeless, did I drivel
    – Being – who?

One who never turned his back but marched breast forward,
    Never doubted clouds would break,
Never dreamed, though right were worsted, wrong would triumph,
Held we fall to rise, are baffled to fight better,
    Sleep to wake.

No, at noonday in the bustle of man's work-time
    Greet the unseen with a cheer!
Bid him forward, breast and back as either should be,
'Strive and thrive!' cry 'Speed, – fight on, fare ever
    There as here!'

by Robert Browning

Sound, Sound the Clarion

Sound, sound the clarion, fill the fife!
Throughout the sensual world proclaim,
One crowded hour of glorious life
Is worth an age without a name.

by Thomas Osbert Mordaunt

Vitaï Lampada

There's a breathless hush in the Close to-night –
Ten to make and the match to win –
A bumping pitch and a blinding light,
An hour to play and the last man in.
And it's not for the sake of a ribboned coat,
Or the selfish hope of a season's fame,
But his Captain's hand on his shoulder smote –
'Play up! play up! and play the game!'

The sand of the desert is sodden red, –
Red with the wreck of a square that broke; –
The Gatling's jammed and the Colonel dead,
And the regiment blind with dust and smoke.
The river of death has brimmed his banks,
And England's far, and Honour a name,
But the voice of a schoolboy rallies the ranks:
'Play up! play up! and play the game!'

This is the word that year by year,
While in her place the School is set,
Every one of her sons must hear,
And none that hears it dare forget.
This they all with a joyful mind
Bear through life like a torch in flame,
And falling fling to the host behind –
'Play up! play up! and play the game!'

by Sir Henry Newbolt

Prospice

Fear death? – to feel the fog in my throat,
The mist in my face,
When the snows begin, and the blasts denote
I am nearing the place,
The power of the night, the press of the storm,
The post of the foe;
Where he stands, the Arch Fear in a visible form,
Yet the strong man must go:
For the journey is done and the summit attained,
And the barriers fall,
Though a battle's to fight ere the guerdon be gained,
The reward of it all.
I was ever a fighter, so – one fight more,
The best and the last!
I would hate that death bandaged my eyes, and forbore,
And bade me creep past.
No! let me taste the whole of it, fare like my peers
The heroes of old,
Bear the brunt, in a minute pay glad life's arrears
Of pain, darkness and cold.
For sudden the worst turns the best to the brave,
The black minute's at end,
And the elements' rage, the fiend-voices that rave,
Shall dwindle, shall blend,
Shall change, shall become first a peace out of pain,
Then a light, then thy breast,
O thou soul of my soul! I shall clasp thee again,
And with God be the rest!

by Robert Browning

Bread and Roses

As we come marching, marching, in the beauty of the day,
A million darkened kitchens, a thousand mill-lofts gray
Are touched with all the radiance that a sudden sun discloses,
For the people hear us singing, 'Bread and Roses, Bread and Roses.'

As we come marching, marching, we battle, too, for men—
For they are women's children and we mother them again.
Our days shall not be sweated from birth until life closes—
Hearts starve as well as bodies: Give us Bread, but give us Roses.

As we come marching, marching, unnumbered women dead
Go crying through our singing their ancient song of Bread;
Small art and love and beauty their trudging spirits knew—
Yes, it is Bread we fight for—but we fight for Roses, too.

As we come marching, marching, we bring the Greater Days—
The rising of the women means the rising of the race.
No more the drudge and idler—ten that toil where one reposes—
But a sharing of life's glories: Bread and Roses, Bread and Roses.

by James Oppenheim

L'Envoi

Stepping onwards, oh, my comrades!
Marching fearless through the darkness,
Marching fearless through the prisons,
With the torch of freedom guiding!

See the face of each is glowing,
Gleaming with the love of freedom;
Gleaming with a selfless triumph,
In the cause of human progress!

Like the pilgrim in the valley,
Enemies may oft assail us,
Enemies may close around us,
Tyrants, hunger, horror, brute-force.

But the glorious dawn is breaking,
Freedom's beauty sheds her radiance;
Freedom's clarion call is sounding,
Rousing all the world to wisdom.

by Emily Wilding Davison

The Women's Litany

Let us in through the guarded gate,
Let us in for our pain's sake!
Lips set smiling and face made fair
Still for you through the pain we bare,
We have hid till our hearts were sore
Blacker things than you ever bore:
Let us in through the guarded gate,
Let us in for our pain's sake!

Let us in through the guarded gate,
Let us in for our strength's sake!
Light held high in a strife ne'er through
We have fought for our sons and you,
We have conquered a million years'
Pain and evil and doubt and tears—
Let us in through the guarded gate,
Let us in for our strength's sake!

Let us in through the guarded gate,
Let us in for your own sake!
We have held you within our hand,
Marred or made as we broke or planned,
We have given you life or killed
King or brute as we taught or willed—
Let us in through the guarded gate,
Let us in for your own sake!

Let us in through the guarded gate,
Let us in for the world's sake!
We are blind who must guide your eyes,
We are weak who must help you rise,
All untaught who must teach and mold
Souls of men till the world is old—
Let us in through the guarded gate,
Let us in for the world's sake!

by Margaret Widdemer

The Masque of Anarchy *(extract)*

LXXIX
'Stand ye calm and resolute,
Like a forest close and mute,
With folded arms and looks which are
Weapons of unvanquished war.

LXXX
'And let Panic, who outspeeds
The career of armèd steeds,
Pass, a disregarded shade,
Through your phalanx undismayed.

LXXXI
'Let the laws of your own land,
Good or ill, between ye stand,
Hand to hand, and foot to foot,
Arbiters of the dispute.

LXXXII
'The old laws of England – they
Whose reverend heads with age are grey,
Children of a wiser day;
And whose solemn voice must be
Thine own echo – Liberty!

LXXXIII
'On those who first should violate
Such sacred heralds in their state
Rest the blood that must ensue,
And it will not rest on you.

LXXXIV

'And if then the tyrants dare
Let them ride among you there,
Slash, and stab, and maim, and hew, –
What they like, that let them do.

LXXXV

'With folded arms and steady eyes,
And little fear, and less surprise,
Look upon them as they slay
Till their rage has died away.

LXXXVI

'Then they will return with shame
To the place from which they came,
And the blood thus shed will speak
In hot blushes on their cheek.

LXXXVII

'Every woman in the land
Will point at them as they stand –
They will hardly dare to greet
Their acquaintance on the street.

LXXXVIII

'And the bold, true warriors
Who have hugged Danger in wars
Will turn to those who would be free,
Ashamed of such base company.

LXXXIX

'And that slaughter to the Nation
Shall steam up like inspiration,
Eloquent, oracular;
A volcano heard afar.

XC

'And these words shall then become
Like Oppression's thundered doom
Ringing through each heart and brain,
Heard again – again – again –

XCI

'Rise like Lions after slumber
In unvanquishable number –
Shake your chains to earth like dew
Which in sleep had fallen on you –
Ye are many – they are few.'

by Percy Bysshe Shelley

If We Must Die

If we must die, let it not be like hogs
Hunted and penned in an inglorious spot,
While round us bark the mad and hungry dogs,
Making their mock at our accursèd lot.
If we must die, O let us nobly die,
So that our precious blood may not be shed
In vain; then even the monsters we defy
Shall be constrained to honor us though dead!
O kinsmen! we must meet the common foe!
Though far outnumbered let us show us brave,
And for their thousand blows deal one death-blow!
What though before us lies the open grave?
Like men we'll face the murderous, cowardly pack,
Pressed to the wall, dying, but fighting back!

by Claude McKay

The Ballad which Anne Askew made and Sang when She was in Newgate

Like as the armed knight
Appointed to the field,
With this world will I fight,
And faith shall be my shield.

Faith is that weapon strong,
Which will not fail at need;
My foes, therefore, among
Therewith will I proceed.

Thou sayst, lord, whoso knock,
To them wilt thou attend,
Undo, therefore, the lock,
And thy strong power send.

More enemies now I have
Than hairs upon my head;
Let them not me deprave
But fight thou in my stead.

Not oft I used to write
In prose, nor yet in rhyme;
Yet will I show one sight,
That I saw in my time:

I saw a royal throne,
Where Justice should have sit;
But in her stead was one
Of moody, cruel wit.

Absorpt was rightwiseness,
As by the raging flood;
Satan, in his excess,
Sucked up the guiltless blood.

Then thought I, – Jesus, Lord,
When thou shalt judge us all,
Hard is it to record
On these men what will fall!

Yet, Lord, I thee desire,
For that they do to me,
Let them not taste the hire
Of their iniquity.

by Anne Askew

And Death Shall Have No Dominion

And death shall have no dominion.
Dead men naked they shall be one
With the man in the wind and the west moon;
When their bones are picked clean and the clean bones gone,
They shall have stars at elbow and foot;
Though they go mad they shall be sane,
Though they sink through the sea they shall rise again;
Though lovers be lost love shall not;
And death shall have no dominion.

And death shall have no dominion.
Under the windings of the sea
They lying long shall not die windily;
Twisting on racks when sinews give way,
Strapped to a wheel, yet they shall not break;
Faith in their hands shall snap in two,
And the unicorn evils run them through;
Split all ends up they shan't crack;
And death shall have no dominion.

And death shall have no dominion.
No more may gulls cry at their ears
Or waves break loud on the seashores;
Where blew a flower may a flower no more
Lift its head to the blows of the rain;
Though they be mad and dead as nails,
Heads of the characters hammer through daisies;
Break in the sun till the sun breaks down,
And death shall have no dominion.

by Dylan Thomas

Hymn

Sung at the completion of the Concord Monument, April 19th, 1836

By the rude bridge that arched the flood,
    Their flag to April's breeze unfurled,
Here once the embattled farmers stood,
    And fired the shot heard round the world.

The foe long since in silence slept;
    Alike the conqueror silent sleeps;
And Time the ruined bridge has swept
    Down the dark stream which seaward creeps.

On this green bank, by this soft stream,
    We set to-day a votive stone;
That memory may their deed redeem,
    When, like our sires, our sons are gone.

Spirit, that made those heroes dare
    To die, and leave their children free,
Bid Time and Nature gently spare
    The shaft we raise to them and thee.

by Ralph Waldo Emerson

Introspective

I wish it were over, the terrible pain,
Pang after pang, again and again;
First the shattering ruining blow,
Then the probing steady and slow.

Did I wince? I did not faint:
My soul broke but was not bent:
Up I stand like a blasted tree
By the shore of the shivering sea.

On my boughs neither leaf nor fruit,
No sap in my utmost root,
Brooding in an anguish dumb
On the short past and the long to-come.

Dumb I was when the ruin fell,
Dumb I remain and will never tell;
O my soul, I talk with thee,
But not another the sight must see.

I did not start when the torture stung,
I did not faint when the torture wrung;
Let it come tenfold if come it must,
But I will not groan when I bite the dust.

by Christina Rossetti

Invictus

Out of the night that covers me,
    Black as the Pit from pole to pole,
I thank whatever gods may be
    For my unconquerable soul.

In the fell clutch of circumstance
    I have not winced nor cried aloud.
Under the bludgeonings of chance
    My head is bloody, but unbowed.

Beyond this place of wrath and tears
    Looms but the Horror of the shade,
And yet the menace of the years
    Finds, and shall find, me unafraid.

It matters not how strait the gate,
    How charged with punishments the scroll,
I am the master of my fate:
    I am the captain of my soul.

by W. E. Henley

From Courage

I was afraid of Fear,
    Not of the foe;
And when I thought that those I hold most dear
    My craven soul would know
And turn away ashamed, who praised before,
    Ashamed and deep distressed to find it so,
I was afraid the more.

Lo, when I joined the fight,
    And bared my breast
To all the darts of that wild, hellish night,
    I, only, stood the test,
For Fear, which I had feared, deserved then,
    And forward blithely at the foe I prest
King of myself again ....

by J. E. Stewart

Goal *(extract)*

I will shatter the wall
Of darkness that rises
From gleaming day
And seeks to hide the sun.
I will turn this wall of
Darkness (that is night)
Into a thing of beauty.

by Mae Cowdery

Do Not Go Gentle into That Good Night

Do not go gentle into that good night,
Old age should burn and rave at close of day;
Rage, rage against the dying of the light.

Though wise men at their end know dark is right,
Because their words had forked no lightning they
Do not go gentle into that good night.

Good men, the last wave by, crying how bright
Their frail deeds might have danced in a green bay,
Rage, rage against the dying of the light.

Wild men who caught and sang the sun in flight,
And learn, too late, they grieved it on its way,
Do not go gentle into that good night.

Grave men, near death, who see with blinding sight
Blind eyes could blaze like meteors and be gay,
Rage, rage against the dying of the light.

And you, my father, there on the sad height,
Curse, bless, me now with your fierce tears, I pray.
Do not go gentle into that good night.
Rage, rage against the dying of the light.

by Dylan Thomas

To Fight Aloud is Very Brave

To fight aloud, is very brave -
But *gallanter*, I know
Who charge within the bosom
The Cavalry of Wo -

Who win, and nations do not see -
Who fall - and none observe -
Whose dying eyes, no Country
Regards with patriot love -

We trust, in plumed procession
For such, the Angels go -
Rank after Rank, with even feet -
And Uniforms of snow.

by Emily Dickinson

Wind Rising in the Alleys

Wind rising in the alleys

My spirit lifts in yours like a banner

Streaming free of hot walls.

You are full of unspent dreams ...

You are laden with beginnings ...

There is hope in you ... not sweet ...

acrid as blood in the mouth.

Come into my tossing dust

Scattering the peace of old deaths,

Wind rising in the alleys,

Carrying stuff of flame.

by Lola Ridge

Protest

To sin by silence, when we should protest,
Makes cowards out of men. The human race
Has climbed on protest. Had no voice been raised
Against injustice, ignorance, and lust,
The inquisition yet would serve the law,
And guillotines decide our least disputes.
The few who dare, must speak and speak again
To right the wrongs of many. Speech, thank God,
No vested power in this great day and land
Can gag or throttle. Press and voice may cry
Loud disapproval of existing ills;
May criticize oppression and condemn
The lawlessness of wealth-protecting laws
That let the children and childbearers toil
To purchase ease for idle millionaires.

Therefore I do protest against the boast
Of independence in this mighty land.
Call no chain strong, which holds one rusted link.
Call no land free, that holds one fettered slave.
Until the manacled slim wrists of babes
Are loosed to toss in childish sport and glee,
Until the mother bears no burden, save
The precious one beneath her heart, until
God's soil is rescued from the clutch of greed
And given back to labor, let no man
Call this the land of freedom.

by Ella Wheeler Wilcox

To a Foil'd European Revolutionaire *(extract)*

Courage yet! my brother or my sister!
Keep on! Liberty is to be subserv'd, whatever occurs;
That is nothing, that is quell'd by one or two failures,
  or any number of failures,
Or by the indifference or ingratitude of the people, or by
  any unfaithfulness,
Or the show of the tushes of power, soldiers, cannon, penal statutes.

Revolt! and still revolt! revolt!
What we believe in waits latent forever through all the continents,
  and all the islands and archipelagos of the sea;
What we believe in invites no one, promises nothing, sits in calmness
  and light, is positive and composed, knows no discouragement,
Waiting patiently, waiting its time.

by Walt Whitman

Courage

Courage is the price that Life exacts for granting peace.

The soul that knows it not knows no release
From little things:

Knows not the livid loneliness of **FEAR**,
Nor mountain heights where bitter joy can hear
The sound of wings.

How can life grant us boon of living, compensate
For dull gray ugliness and pregnant hate
Unless we ***dare***

The soul's dominion? Each time we make a choice, *we pay*
With courage to behold the resistless day,
And count it FAIR.

by Amelia Earhart

Consolation

When raging love with extreme pain
    Most cruelly distrains my heart,
When that my tears, as floods of rain,
    Bear witness of my woeful smart;
        When sighs have wasted so my breath
        That I lie at the point of death,

I call to mind the navy great
    That the Greeks brought to Troyé town,
And how the boisterous winds did beat
    Their ships, and rent their sails adown;
        Till Agamemnon's daughter's blood
        Appeased the Gods that them withstood.

And how that in those ten years' war
    Full many a bloody deed was done,
And many a lord that came full far,
    There caught his bane, alas! too soon;
        And many a good knight overrun,
        Before the Greeks had Helen won.

Then think I thus: sith such repair,
    So long time war of valiant men,
Was all to win a lady fair,
    Shall I not learn to suffer then,
        And think my life well spent to be,
        Serving a worthier wight than she?

Therefore I never will repent,
    But pains contented still endure;
For like as when, rough winter spent,
    The pleasant spring straight draweth in ure,
        So, after raging storms of care,
        Joyful at length may be my fare.

by Henry Howard, Earl of Surrey

Escape

When we get out of the glass bottles of our own ego,
and when we escape like squirrels from turning in the cages
  of our personality
and get into the forest again,
we shall shiver with cold and fright
but things will happen to us
so that we don't know ourselves.

Cool, unlying life will rush in,
and passion will make our bodies taut with power,
we shall stamp our feet with new power
and old things will fall down,
we shall laugh, and institutions will curl up like burnt paper.

by D. H. Lawrence

The Adventurous Muse *(extract)*

Give me the chariot whose diviner wheels
    Mark their own route, and unconfined
    Bound o'er the everlasting hills,
And lose the clouds below, and leave the stars behind.
    Give me the Muse whose generous force
        Impatient of the reins
    Pursues an unattempted course,
    Breaks all the critic's iron chains,
And bears to paradise the raptured mind.

by Isaac Watts

The Golden Journey to Samarkand *(extract)*

We are the Pilgrims, master; we shall go
Always a little further: it may be
Beyond that last blue mountain barred with snow,
Across that angry or that glimmering sea,

White on a throne or guarded in a cave
There lives a prophet who can understand
Why men were born: but surely we are brave,
Who make the Golden Journey to Samarkand.

by James Elroy Flecker

Valiant-for-Truth's Description of a Pilgrim
(extract from The Pilgrim's Progress*)*

Who would true valour see,
Let him come hither;
One here will constant be,
Come wind, come weather.
There's no discouragement
Shall make him once relent
His first avow'd intent
To be a pilgrim.

Whoso beset him round
With dismal stories,
Do but themselves confound,
His strength the more is.
No lion can him fright,
He'll with a giant fight,
But he will have a right
To be a pilgrim.

Hobgoblin, nor foul fiend,
Can daunt his spirit;
He knows he at the end
Shall life inherit.
Then fancies fly away,
He'll fear not what men say,
He'll labour night and day
To be a pilgrim.

by John Bunyan

Eldorado

Gaily bedight,
A gallant knight,
In sunshine and in shadow,
Had journeyed long,
Singing a song,
In search of Eldorado.

But he grew old—
This knight so bold—
And o'er his heart a shadow—
Fell as he found
No spot of ground
That looked like Eldorado.

And, as his strength
Failed him at length,
He met a pilgrim shadow—
'Shadow,' said he,
'Where can it be—
This land of Eldorado?'

'Over the Mountains
Of the Moon,
Down the Valley of the Shadow,
Ride, boldly ride,'
The shade replied,—
'If you seek for Eldorado!'

by Edgar Allan Poe

Death Stands Above Me

Death stands above me, WHISPERING LOW
I know not what into my ear;
Of his STRANGE LANGUAGE all I know
Is, there is not a word of FEAR.

by Walter Savage Landor

CHAPTER FOUR

The Power is Yours

"Yours is the Earth and everything that's in it"

If
Rudyard Kipling

To Praise the Mutilated World

Try to praise the mutilated world.
Remember June's long days,
and wild strawberries, drops of rosé wine.
The nettles that methodically overgrow
the abandoned homesteads of exiles.
You must praise the mutilated world.
You watched the stylish yachts and ships;
one of them had a long trip ahead of it,
while salty oblivion awaited others.
You've seen the refugees going nowhere,
you've heard the executioners sing joyfully.
You should praise the mutilated world.
Remember the moments when we were together
in a white room and the curtain fluttered.
Return in thought to the concert where music flared.
You gathered acorns in the park in autumn
and leaves eddied over the earth's scars.
Praise the mutilated world
and the gray feather a thrush lost,
and the gentle light that strays and vanishes
and returns.

by Adam Zagajewski
(translated by Clare Cavanagh)

Locked Inside

She beats upon her bolted door,
    With faint weak hands;
Drearily walks the narrow floor;
Sullenly sits, blank walls before;
    Despairing stands.

Life calls her, Duty, Pleasure, Gain –
    Her dreams respond;
But the blank daylights wax and wane,
Dull peace, sharp agony, slow pain –
    No hope beyond.

Till she comes a thought! She lifts her head,
    The world grows wide!
A voice – as if clear words were said –
'Your door, O long imprisonéd,
    Is locked inside!'

by Charlotte Perkins Gilman

Lift Every Voice and Sing

Lift every voice and sing
Till earth and heaven ring,
Ring with the harmonies of Liberty;
Let our rejoicing rise
High as the listening skies,
Let it resound loud as the rolling sea.
Sing a song full of the faith that the dark
        past has taught us,
Sing a song full of the hope that the present
        has brought us.
Facing the rising sun of our new day begun,
Let us march on till victory is won.

Stony the road we trod,
Bitter the chastening rod,
Felt in the days when hope unborn had died;
Yet with a steady beat,
Have not our weary feet
Come to the place for which our fathers sighed?
We have come over a way that with tears has
        been watered,
We have come, treading our path through the blood
        of the slaughtered,
Out from the gloomy past,
Till now we stand at last
Where the white gleam of our bright star is cast.

God of our weary years,
God of our silent tears,
Thou who hast brought us thus far on the way;
Thou who hast by Thy might
Led us into the light,
Keep us forever in the path, we pray.
Lest our feet stray from the places, our God,
    where we met Thee,
Lest, our hearts drunk with the wine of the world,
    we forget Thee;
Shadowed beneath Thy hand,
May we forever stand.
True to our God,
True to our native land.

by James Weldon Johnson

If –

If you can keep your head when all about you
Are losing theirs and blaming it on you,
If you can trust yourself when all men doubt you,
But make allowance for their doubting too;
If you can wait and not be tired by waiting,
Or being lied about, don't deal in lies,
Or being hated, don't give way to hating,
And yet don't look too good, nor talk too wise:
If you can dream – and not make dreams your master;
If you can think – and not make thoughts your aim;
If you can meet with Triumph and Disaster
And treat those two impostors just the same;
If you can bear to hear the truth you've spoken
Twisted by knaves to make a trap for fools,
Or watch the things you gave your life to, broken,
And stoop and build 'em up with worn-out tools:

If you can make one heap of all your winnings
And risk it on one turn of pitch-and-toss,
And lose, and start again at your beginnings
And never breathe a word about your loss;
If you can force your heart and nerve and sinew
To serve your turn long after they are gone,
And so hold on when there is nothing in you
Except the Will which says to them: 'Hold on!'

If you can talk with crowds and keep your virtue,
Or walk with Kings – nor lose the common touch,
If neither foes nor loving friends can hurt you,
If all men count with you, but none too much;
If you can fill the unforgiving minute
With sixty seconds' worth of distance run,
Yours is the Earth and everything that's in it,
And – which is more – you'll be a Man, my son!

by Rudyard Kipling

The Guest House

This being human is a guest house,
Every morning a new arrival.

A joy, a depression, a meanness,
some momentary awareness comes
as an unexpected visitor.

Welcome and entertain them all!
Even if they're a crowd of sorrows,
who violently sweep your house
empty of its furniture,
still, treat each guest honourably.
He may be clearing you out for some new delight.

The dark thought, the shame, the malice,
meet them at the door laughing,
and invite them in.

Be grateful for whoever comes,
because each has been sent
as a guide from beyond.

by Rumi
(translated by Reynold A. Nicholson)

The Winds of Fate

One ship drives east and another drives west

With the selfsame winds that blow.

'Tis the set of the sails

And not of the gales

Which tells us the way to go.

Like the winds of the sea are the ways of fate,

As we voyage along through life;

'Tis the set of the soul

That decides its goal

And not the CALM or the STRIFE.

by Ella Wheeler Wilcox

A Farewel to Worldly Joyes

Farewel to Unsubstantial Joyes,
Ye Gilded Nothings, Gaudy Toyes,
Too long ye have my Soul misled,
Too long with Aiery Diet fed:
But now my Heart ye shall no more
Deceive, as you have heretofore:
For when I hear such *Sirens* sing,
Like *Ithicas*'s fore-warned King,
With prudent Resolution I
Will so my Will and Fancy tye,
That stronger to the Mast not he,
Than I to Reason bound will be:
And though your Witchcrafts strike my Ear,
Unhurt, like him, your Charms I'll hear.

by Anne Killigrew

Variation on a Theme by Rilke

A certain day became a presence to me;
there it was, confronting me – a sky, air, light:
a being. And before it started to descend
from the height of noon, it leaned over
and struck my shoulder as if with
the flat of a sword, granting me
honor and a task. The day's blow
rang out, metallic – or it was I, a bell awakened,
and what I heard was my whole self
saying and singing what it knew: I can.

by Denise Levertov

The Secret

In the profoundest Ocean
There is a rainbow shell,
It is always there, shining most stilly
Under the greatest storm waves
And under the happy little waves
That the old Greek called 'ripples of laughter.'
And you listen, the rainbow shell
Sings in the profoundest ocean —
It is always there, singing most silently ..!

by Katherine Mansfield

Inventory

Four be the things I am wiser to know:
Idleness, sorrow, a friend, and a foe.

Four be the things I'd been better without:
Love, curiosity, freckles, and doubt.

Three be the things I shall never attain:
Envy, content, and sufficient champagne.

Three be the things I shall have till I die:
Laughter and hope and a sock in the eye.

by Dorothy Parker

A Psalm of Life *(extract)*

Lives of great men all remind us
    We can make our lives sublime,
And, departing, leave behind us
    Footprints on the sands of time;

Footprints, that perhaps another,
    Sailing o'er life's solemn main,
A forlorn and shipwrecked brother,
    Seeing, shall take heart again.

Let us, then, be up and doing,
    With a heart for any fate;
Still achieving, still pursuing,
    Learn to labour and to wait.

by Henry Wadsworth Longfellow

To Toussaint L'Ouverture *(extract)*

Yet die not; do thou
Wear rather in thy bonds a cheerful brow:
Though fallen thyself, never to rise again,
Live, and take comfort. Thou hast left behind
Powers that will work for thee; air, earth, and skies;
There's not a breathing of the common wind
That will forget thee; thou hast great allies;
Thy friends are exultations, agonies,
And love, and man's unconquerable mind.

by William Wordsworth

Happy Thought

The world is so full
of a
number of
things,
I'm sure we should all be as happy as kings.

by Robert Louis Stevenson

The Washing

The washing never gets done.
The furnace never gets heated.
Books never get read.
Life is never completed.
Life is like a ball which one must continually
catch and hit so it won't fall.
When the fence is repaired at one end,
it collapses on the other. The roof leaks,
the kitchen door won't close, there are cracks in the foundation,
the torn knees of children's pants ...
One can't keep everything in mind. The wonder is
that beside all this one can notice
the spring which is so full of everything
continuing in all directions – into the evening clouds,
into the redwing's song and into every
drop of dew on every blade of grass in the meadow,
as far as the eye can see, into the dusk.

by Jaan Kaplinski

To Althea, From Prison

When Love with unconfinèd wings
Hovers within my gates,
And my divine Althea brings
To whisper at the grates;
When I lie tangled in her hair
And fettered to her eye,
The gods that wanton in the air,
Know no such liberty.

When flowing cups run swiftly round,
With no allaying Thames,
Our careless heads with roses bound,
Our hearts with loyal flames;
When thirsty grief in wine we steep,
When healths and draughts go free,
Fishes, that tipple in the deep,
Know no such liberty.

When, like committed linnets, I
With shriller throat shall sing
The sweetness, mercy, majesty,
And glories of my King;
When I shall voice aloud how good
He is, how great should be,
Enlargèd winds, that curl the flood,
Know no such liberty.

Stone walls do not a prison make,
Nor iron bars a cage;
Minds innocent and quiet take
That for an hermitage.
If I have freedom in my love,
And in my soul am free,
Angels alone, that soar above,
Enjoy such liberty.

by Richard Lovelace

The Great Lover *(extract)*

I have been so great a lover: filled my days
So proudly with the splendour of Love's praise,
The pain, the calm, and the astonishment,
Desire illimitable, and still content,
And all dear names men use, to cheat despair,
For the perplexed and viewless streams that bear
Our hearts at random down the dark of life.
Now, ere the unthinking silence on that strife
Steals down, I would cheat drowsy Death so far,
My night shall be remembered for a star
That outshone all the suns of all men's days.

by Rupert Brooke

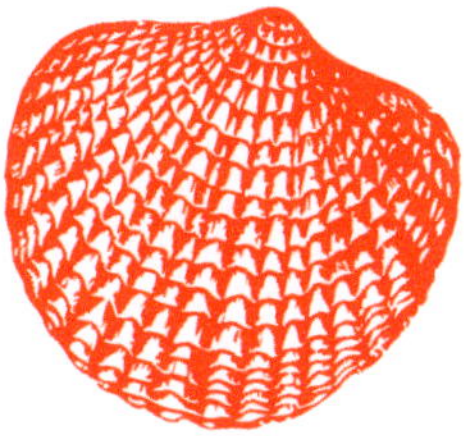

Boxing Day Swimmers

It's the strangest thing, lately,
I open my mouth and my mother falls out –
a mournful clockwork woodpigeon on the kitchen table.

After lunch we drag the children along the seafront.
My god, let me be like those women, bobble hatted
and wobbling towards high tide. Those women,
salt brined, making joyous hams of their bodies.
On delicate, brittle days, bring me to the shore.
Show me how to punch the cold
right in the centre of its stupid face.

by Jen Feroze

Happy the Man *(extract)*

Happy the man, and happy he alone,
he who can call today his own:
he who, secure within, can say,
Tomorrow do thy worst, for I have lived today.

by Horace (Quintus Horatius Flaccus)
(translated by John Dryden)

Thinking

If you think you are beaten, you are;
    If you think you dare not, you don't.
If you'd like to win, but think you can't,
    It's almost a cinch you won't.

If you think you'll lose, you're lost,
    For out of the world we find
Success begins with a fellow's will –
    It's all in the state of mind.

If you think you're outclassed, you are;
    You've got to think high to rise;
You've got to be sure of yourself before
    You can ever win a prize.

Life's battles don't always go
    To the stronger or faster man;
But soon or late the man who wins,
    Is the one who *thinks he can.*

by Walter D. Wintle

Kingdom

My mind to me a kingdom is,
  Such present joys therein I find,
That it excels all other bliss
  That world affords or grows by kind.
Though much I want which most would have,
Yet still my mind forbids to crave.

No princely pomp, no wealthy store,
  No force to win the victory,
No wily wit to salve a sore,
  No shape to win a loving eye;
To none of these I yield as thrall,
For why my mind doth serve for all.

I see how plenty suffers oft,
  And hasty climbers soon do fall;
I see that those which are aloft
  Mishap doth threaten most of all;
They get with toil, and keep with fear:
Such cares my mind could never bear.

Content I live, this is my stay,
  I seek no more than may suffice;
I press to bear no haughty sway;
  Look, what I lack my mind supplies.
Lo! thus I triumph like a king,
Content with that my mind doth bring.

Some have too much, yet still do crave;
  I have little, and seek no more.
They are but poor, though much they have,
  And I am rich with little store.
They poor, I rich; they beg, I give;
They lack, I leave; they pine, I live.

I laugh not at another's loss;
  I grudge not at another's gain;
No worldly waves my mind can toss;
  My state at one doth still remain.
I fear no foe, I fawn no friend;
I loathe not life, nor dread my end.

Some weigh their pleasure by their lust,
  Their wisdom by their rage of will;
Their treasure is their only trust,
  A cloaked craft their store of skill:
But all the pleasure that I find
Is to maintain a quiet mind.

My wealth is health and perfect ease,
  My conscience clear my choice defence;
I neither seek by bribes to please,
  Nor by deceit to breed offence.
Thus do I live; thus will I die;
Would all did so as well as I!

by Sir Edward Dyer

Old Song

Do not seek too much *fame*,

but do not seek *obscurity*.

BE PROUD,

But do not remind the world of your deeds.

EXCEL WHEN YOU MUST,

but do not excel the world,

MANY HEROES ARE NOT YET BORN,

many have already *died*.

To be alive to hear this song is a *victory*.

by Anon. (traditional, West Africa)

Character of a Happy Life

How happy is he born and taught
That serveth not another's will;
Whose armour is his honest thought
And simple truth his utmost skill!

Whose passions not his masters are,
Whose soul is still prepared for death,
Not tied unto the world by care
Of public fame, or private breath;

Who envies none that chance doth raise
Or vice; Who never understood
How deepest wounds are given by praise;
Nor rules of state, but rules of good:

Who hath his life from rumours freed,
Whose conscience is his strong retreat;
Whose state can neither flatterers feed,
Nor ruin make accusers great;

Who God doth late and early pray
More of his grace than gifts to lend;
And entertains the harmless day
With a well-chosen book or friend;

—This man is freed from servile bands
Of hope to rise, or fear to fall;
Lord of himself, though not of lands;
And having nothing, yet hath all.

by Sir Henry Wotton

Why in the World

Why in the world do you want to **CARRY**

Things that annoy and harass and **HARRY?**

STOP THEM AND DROP THEM, a new day is here,

SQUEEZE A LAUGH FROM IT instead of a tear.

by Herbert Kaufman

On Myself

Good Heav'n, I thank thee, since it was designed
I should be framed, but of the weaker kind,
That yet, my Soul, is rescued from the love
Of all those trifles which their passions move.
Pleasures and praise and plenty have with me
But their just value. If allowed they be,
Freely, and thankfully as much I taste,
As will not reason or religion waste.
If they're denied, I on my self can live,
And slight those aids unequal chance does give.
When in the sun, my wings can be displayed,
And, in retirement, I can bless the shade.

by Anne Finch, Countess of Winchilsea

Careless Content *(extract)*

I am content, I do not care,
    Wag as it will the world for me;
When fuss and fret was all my fare,
    It got no ground, as I could see:
So when away my caring went,
I counted cost, and was content.

With more of thanks, and less of thought,
    I strive to make my matters meet;
To seek what ancient sages sought,
    Physic and food, in sour and sweet:
To take what passes in good part,
And keep the hiccups from the heart.

With good and gentle-humoured hearts,
    I choose to chat where'er I come,
Whate'er the subject be that starts;
    But if I get among the glum,
I hold my tongue to tell the troth,
And keep my breath to cool my broth.

For chance or change, of peace or pain,
    For Fortune's favour or her frown;
For lack or glut, for loss or gain,
    I never dodge, nor up nor down:
But swing what way the ship shall swim,
Or tack about with equal trim.

I suit not where I shall not speed,
    Nor trace the turn of ev'ry tide;
If simple sense will not succeed,
    I made no bustling, but abide:
For shining wealth or scaring woe,
I force no friend, I fear no foe.

by John Byrom

When in the Dumps

Don't be sorry for yourself—better smile.
Worst of troubles will disperse—in a while.
If self-pity mounts up high,
you are bound to mope or cry,
bound to amplify your trouble,
make it grow in size, quite double,
being sorry for oneself is out of style!

Don't be sorry for yourself—better smile;
blackest clouds will pass away—in a while.
'Tis true, you've been hard hit,
not a friend but would admit
you have cause to lose some sleep,
quite a lot to make you weep.
Don't you do it, though, for pity's out of style!

Don't be sorry for yourself—better smile.
Sun and moon and stars will shine—in a while,
and self-pity doesn't pay, for it has a nasty way
of turning courage pale, and then we're bound to fail.
So let's toss our heads and laugh;
lo! the troubles fade to half.
Just keep smiling—for self-pity's out of style!

by Wilhelmina Stitch

The Resolve *(extract)*

For what the world admires I'll wish no more,
Nor court that airy nothing of a name:
Such flitting shadows let the proud adore,
Let them be suppliants for an empty fame.

If Reason rules within, and keeps the throne,
While the inferior faculties obey,
And all her laws without reluctance own,
Accounting none more fit, more just than they;

If Virtue my free soul unsullied keeps,
Exempting it from passion and from stain,
If no black guilty thoughts disturb my sleeps,
And no past crimes my vexed remembrance pain;

If, though I pleasure find in living here,
I yet can look on death without surprise;
If I've a soul above the reach of fear,
And which will nothing mean or sordid prize;

Then am I happy in my humble state,
Although not crowned with glory nor with bays:
A mind, that triumphs over vice and fate,
Esteems it mean to court the world for praise.

by Mary, Lady Chudleigh

My Life's Stem Was Cut

My life's stem was cut,
But quickly, lovingly
I was lifted up,
I heard the rush of the tap
And I was set in water
In the blue vase, beautiful
In lip and curve,
And here I am
Opening one petal
As the tea cools.
I wait while the sun moves
And the bees finish their dancing,
I know I am dying
But why not keep flowering
As long as I can
From my cut stem?

by Helen Dunmore

Faith

I keep a bird in my heart,
He lives on sorrow,
His name is Faith.
He is so quick a conjurer that he can borrow
Flesh from a wraith.

He swallows the harsh weeds of pain
And gives me scope,
To tend my little garden-plot again
And wait for Hope.

by Anna Wickham

Dancing with Life

I beckoned to the floor
missed buses and lost races.
We body-popped till sore.

I held out my hand
to every failed exam.
We lindy-hopped. We can-canned.

I slipped my arm around the waist
of *chicken, loser, nerd.*
We skip-jived at a pace.

I chose the longest dullest week
and pressed it to my chest
as we cha-cha'd cheek to cheek.

I tipped and doffed my hat
to a hundred horrid haircuts.
We mambo'd, tango'd, tapped.

Feeling bold, I turned to face
my darkest, rawest faults.
I took them in my arms. We bowed
and broke into a waltz.

by Shauna Darling Robertson

Eternity

He who binds to himself a joy
Does the winged life destroy;
But he who kisses the joy as it flies
Lives in eternity's sunrise.

by William Blake

A Prayer

Lord make me an
instrument of Thy peace.
Where there is hatred,
Let me sow love;
Where there is injury,
Let me sow pardon;
Where there is doubt, faith;
Where there is despair, hope;
Where there is darkness, light;
Where there is sadness, joy.
(Amen)

by St Francis of Assisi

If You Look for the Truth Outside Yourself

If you look for the truth outside yourself,
it gets farther and farther away.
Today, walking alone,
I meet him everywhere I step.
He is the same as me,
yet, I am not him.
Only if you understand it in this way
will you merge
with the way things are.

by Tung-Shan

Comrades

I and my Soul are alone to-day,
    All in the shining weather;
We were sick of the world, and we put it away,
    So we could rejoice together.

Our host, the Sun, in the blue, blue sky,
    Is mixing a rare, sweet wine,
In the burnished gold of his cup on high,
    For me, and this Soul of mine.

We find it a safe and a royal drink,
    And a cure for every pain:
It helps us to love, and helps us to think,
    And strengthens body and brain.

And sitting here, with my Soul alone,
    Where the yellow sun-rays fall,
Of all the friends I have ever known
    I find it the *best* of all.

We rarely meet when the World is near,
    For the World hath a pleasing art,
And brings me so much that is bright and dear
    That my Soul it keepeth apart.

But when I grow weary of mirth and glee,
    Of glitter, glow, and splendour,
Like a tried old friend it comes to me
    With a smile that is sad and tender.

And we walk together as two friends may,
    And laugh, and drink God's wine.
Oh, a royal comrade any day,
    I find this Soul of mine.

by Ella Wheeler Wilcox

To Imagination

When weary with the long day's care,
And earthly change from pain to pain,
And lost, and ready to despair,
Thy kind voice calls me back again—
O my true friend, I am not lone
While thou canst speak with such a tone!

So hopeless is the world without,
The world within I doubly prize;
Thy world where guile and hate and doubt
And cold suspicion never rise;
Where thou and I and Liberty
Have undisputed sovereignty.

What matters it that all around
Danger and grief and darkness lie,
If but within our bosom's bound
We hold a bright unsullied sky,
Warm with ten thousand mingled rays
Of suns that know no winter days?

Reason indeed may oft complain
For Nature's sad reality,
And tell the suffering heart how vain
Its cherished dreams must always be;
And Truth may rudely trample down
The flowers of Fancy newly blown.

But thou art ever there to bring
The hovering visions back and breathe
New glories o'er the blighted spring
And call a lovelier life from death,
And whisper with a voice divine
Of real worlds as bright as thine.

I trust not to thy phantom bliss,
Yet still in evening's quiet hour
With never-failing thankfulness
I welcome thee, benignant power,
Sure solacer of human cares
And brighter hope when hope despairs.

by Emily Brontë

Imagination

There is a dish to hold the sea,
    A brazier to contain the sun,
A compass for the galaxy,
    A voice to wake the dead and done!

That minister of ministers,
    Imagination, gathers up
The undiscovered Universe,
    Like jewels in a jasper cup.

Its flame can mingle north and south;
    Its accent with the thunder strive;
The ruddy sentence of its mouth
    Can make the ancient dead alive.

The mart of power, the fount of will,
    The form and mould of every star,
The source and bound of good and ill,
    The key of all the things that are,

Imagination, new and strange
    In every age, can turn the year;
Can shift the poles and lightly change
    The mood of men, the world's career.

by John Davidson

The Gift to Sing

Sometimes the mist overhangs my path,
And blackening clouds about me cling;
But, oh, I have a magic way
To turn the gloom to cheerful day—
    I softly sing.

And if the way grows darker still,
Shadowed by Sorrow's somber wing,
With glad defiance in my throat,
I pierce the darkness with a note,
    And sing, and sing.

I brood not over the broken past,
Nor dread whatever time may bring;
No nights are dark, no days are long,
While in my heart there swells a song,
    And I can sing.

by James Weldon Johnson

The Poet and His Song

A song is but a little thing,
And yet what joy it is to sing!
In hours of toil it gives me zest,
And when at eve I long for rest;
When cows come home along the bars,
And in the fold I hear the bell,
As Night, the shepherd, herds his stars,
I sing my song, and all is well.

There are no ears to hear my lays,
No lips to lift a word of praise;
But still, with faith unfaltering,
I live and laugh and love and sing.
What matters yon unheeding throng?
They cannot feel my spirit's spell,
Since life is sweet and love is long,
I sing my song, and all is well.

My days are never days of ease;
I till my ground and prune my trees.
When ripened gold is all the plain,
I put my sickle to the grain.
I labour hard, and toil and sweat,
While others dream within the dell;
But even while my brow is wet,
I sing my song, and all is well.

Sometimes the sun, unkindly hot,
My garden makes a desert spot;
Sometimes a blight upon the tree
Takes all my fruit away from me;
And then with throes of bitter pain
Rebellious passions rise and swell;
But – life is more than fruit or grain,
And so I sing, and all is well.

by Paul Laurence Dunbar

Pack Up Your Troubles in Your Old Kit Bag

Pack up your troubles in your old kit-bag
And smile, smile, smile,
Don't let your joy and laughter hear the snag,
Smile, boys, that's the style.
What's the use of worrying?
It never was worthwhile
So pack up your troubles in your old kit-bag
And smile, smile, smile.

by George Henry Powell

Just Whistle a Bit *(extract)*

Just whistle a bit, if the night be drear
    And the stars refuse to shine:
And a gleam that mocks the starlight clear
    Within you glows benign.

Till the dearth of light in the glooming skies
Is lost to the sight of your soul-lit eyes.
What matters the absence of moon or star?
The light within is the best by far.

by Paul Laurence Dunbar

Be Like the Bird

Be like the bird, who
Resting in his flight
On a twig too slight
Feels it bend beneath him
Yet sings,
Knowing he has wings.

by Victor Hugo

Songs for the People

Let me make the songs for the people,
Songs for the old and young;
Songs to stir like a battle-cry
Wherever they are sung.

Not for the clashing of sabres,
For carnage nor for strife;
But songs to thrill the hearts of men
With more abundant life.

Let me make the songs for the weary,
Amid life's fever and fret,
Till hearts shall relax their tension,
And careworn brows forget.

Let me sing for little children,
Before their footsteps stray,
Sweet anthems of love and duty,
To float o'er life's highway.

I would sing for the poor and aged,
    When shadows dim their sight;
Of the bright and restful mansions,
    Where there shall be no night.

Our world, so worn and weary,
    Needs music, pure and strong,
To hush the jangle and discords
    Of sorrow, pain, and wrong.

Music to soothe all its sorrow,
    Till war and crime shall cease;
And the hearts of men grown tender
    Girdle the world with peace.

by Frances Ellen Watkins Harper

A House Called Tomorrow

You are not fifteen, or twelve, or seventeen—
You are a hundred wild centuries

And fifteen, bringing with you
In every breath and in every step

Everyone who has come before you,
All the yous that you have been,

The mothers of your mother,
The fathers of your father.

If someone in your family tree was trouble,
A hundred were not:

The bad do not win—not finally,
No matter how loud they are.

We simply would not be here
If that were so.

You are made, fundamentally, from the good.
With this knowledge, you never march alone.

You are the breaking news of the century.
You are the good who has come forward

Through it all, even if so many days
Feel otherwise. But think:

When you as a child learned to speak,
It's not that you didn't know words—

It's that, from the centuries, you knew so many,
And it's hard to choose the words that will be your own.

From those centuries we human beings bring with us
The simple solutions and songs,

The river bridges and star charts and song harmonies
All in service to a simple idea:

That we can make a house called tomorrow.
What we bring, finally, into the new day, every day,

Is ourselves. And that's all we need
To start. That's everything we require to keep going.

Look back only for as long as you must,
Then go forward into the history you will make.

Be good, then better. Write books. Cure disease.
Make us proud. Make yourself proud.

And those who came before you? When you hear thunder,
Hear it as their applause.

by Alberto Ríos

The Brave

The brave do never *shun the light;*

Just are their thoughts, and open are their tempers;

Freely without disguise they *love or hate;*

Still are they found in the fair face of day,

And heav'n and men are *judges of their actions.*

by Nicholas Rowe

Up! Quit Thy Bower

UP! quit thy bower, late wears the hour;
Long have the rooks caw'd round thy tower;
On flower and tree, loud hums the bee;
The wilding kid sports merrily:
A day so bright, so fresh, so clear,
Shineth when good fortune's near.

UP! lady fair, and braid thy hair,
And rouse thee in the breezy air;
The lulling stream, that sooth'd thy dream,
Is dancing in the sunny beam:
And hours so sweet, so bright, so gay,
Will waft good fortune on its way.

UP! time will tell; the friar's bell
Its service sound hath chimed well;
The aged crone keeps house alone,
And reapers to the fields are gone:
The active day, so boon and bright,
May bring good fortune ere the night.

by Joanna Baillie

The Road Not Taken

Two roads diverged in a yellow wood,
And sorry I could not travel both
And be one traveller, long I stood
And looked down one as far as I could
To where it bent in the undergrowth;

Then took the other, as just as fair,
And having perhaps the better claim,
Because it was grassy and wanted wear;
Though as for that, the passing there
Had worn them really about the same,

And both that morning equally lay
In leaves no step had trodden black.
Oh, I kept the first for another day!
Yet knowing how way leads on to way,
I doubted if I should ever come back.

I shall be telling this with a sigh
Somewhere ages and ages hence:
Two roads diverged in a wood, and I –
I took the one less travelled by,
And that has made all the difference.

by Robert Frost

Come to the Edge

Come to the edge.
We might fall.
Come to the edge.
It's too high!
COME TO THE EDGE!
And they came,
and he pushed,
and they flew.

Christopher Logue

High Flight

Oh! I have slipped the surly bonds of Earth
And danced the skies on laughter-silvered wings;
Sunward I've climbed, and joined the tumbling mirth
of sun-split clouds, – and done a hundred things
You have not dreamed of – wheeled and soared and swung
High in the sunlit silence. Hov'ring there,
I've chased the shouting wind along, and flung
My eager craft through footless halls of air ...

Up, up the long, delirious burning blue
I've topped the wind-swept heights with easy grace
Where never lark, or even eagle flew –
And, while with silent, lifting mind I've trod
The high untrespassed sanctity of space,
Put out my hand, and touched the face of God.

by John Gillespie Magee

Lady Windermere's Fan *(extract)*

We are all in the gutter,
but some of us are looking at the stars.

by Oscar Wilde

Note on Will

My will is free,
Yet in control
Of infinite tensions.
In the soul
A moving storm
Is under governance of laws,
Yet free to induce form,
Yet free to cause.

That will is free
I clearly prove,
When will in me
Is felt to move.
Freedom on earth has never absolute existence.
It's power to move,
To overcome degrees of earth's resistance.

The flying bat is free in air,
Since he meets small denial there,
Yet if he flies against the wall
He is refused, and has no liberty at all.
I am given the world which lies rhythmic and still.
I am given hot, climbing fire, and that is will.

by Anna Wickham

The Prelude, Book I *(extract)*

My own voice cheared me, and, far more, the mind's
Internal echo of the imperfect sound;
To both I listened, drawing from them both
A cheerful confidence in things to come.

by William Wordsworth

To My Own Heart *(extract)*

Love all that's fair on earth, or near or far,

Yet deem the fairest but a SHOOTING STAR,

And strive to point his spirit's inward sight,

To orb for ever fixed, FOR EVER BRIGHT;

Mourn countless sins, yet trust to be forgiven,

And feel a hesitating HOPE OF HEAVEN!

by Maria Jane Jewsbury

Beauty

What does it mean? Tired, angry, and ill at ease,
No man, woman, or child alive could please
Me now. And yet I almost dare to laugh
Because I sit and frame an epitaph –
'Here lies all that no one loved of him
And that loved no one.' Then in a trice that whim
Has wearied. But, though I am like a river
At fall of evening while it seems that never
Has the sun lighted it or warmed it, while
Cross breezes cut the surface to a file,
This heart, some fraction of me, happily
Floats through a window even now to a tree
Down in the misting, dim-lit, quiet vale;
Not like a pewit that returns to wail
For something it has lost, but like a dove
That slants unswerving to its home and love.
There I find my rest, and through the dusk air
Flies what yet lives in me. Beauty is there.

by Edward Thomas

A November Daisy

Afterthought of summer's bloom!
Late arrival at the feast,
Coming when the songs have ceased
And the merry guests departed,
Leaving but an empty room,
Silence, solitude, and gloom, –
Are you lonely, heavy-hearted;
You, the last of all your kind,
Nodding in the autumn-wind;
Now that all your friends are flown,
Blooming late and all alone?

Nay, I wrong you, little flower,
Reading mournful mood of mine
In your looks, that give no sign
Of a spirit dark and cheerless!
You possess the heavenly power
That rejoices in the hour.
Glad, contented, free, and fearless,
Lift a sunny face to heaven
When a sunny day is given!
Make a summer of your own,
Blooming late and all alone!

Once the daisies gold and white
Sea-like through the meadow rolled:
Once my heart could hardly hold
All its pleasures. I remember,
In the flood of youth's delight
Separate joys were lost to sight.
That was summer! Now November
Sets the perfect flower apart;
Gives each blossom of the heart
Meaning, beauty, grace unknown, –
Blooming late and all alone.

by Henry Van Dyke

To Make a Prairie

To make a prairie it takes
a clover and
one bee,
One clover, and
a bee.

And revery.
The revery alone
will do,
If bees
are few.

by Emily Dickinson

Suppose *(extract)*

Suppose you're dressed for walking,
    And the rain comes pouring down,
Will it clear off any sooner
    Because you scold and frown?
And wouldn't it be nicer
    For you to smile than pout,
And so make sunshine in the house
    When there is none without?

by Phoebe Cary

Boats in the Bay

I will take my trouble and wrap it in a blue handkerchief
And carry it down to the sea.
The sea is as smooth as silk, is as silent as glass;
It does not even whisper
Only the boats, rowed out by the girls in yellow
Ruffle its surface.
It is grey, not blue. It is flecked with boats like midges,
With happy people
Moving soundlessly over the level water.

I will take my trouble and drop it into the water
It is heavy as stone and smooth as a sea-washed pebble.
It will sink under the sea, and the happy people
Will row over it quietly, ruffling the clear water
Little dark boats like midges, skimming silently
Will pass backwards and forwards, the girls singing;
They will never know that they have sailed above sorrow.
Sink heavily and lie still, lie still my trouble.

by Winifred Holtby

Autumn

I at my window sit, and see
Autumn his russet fingers lay
    On ev'ry leaf of ev'ry tree.
I call, but Summer will not stay.

    She flies, the boasting goddess flies,
And, pointing where th' espaliers shoot,
    'Deserve my parting gift,' she cries,
'I take the leaves but not the fruit.'

    Let me the parting gift improve,
And emulate the just reply,
    As life's short seasons swift remove,
Ere fixed in Winter's frost I lie.

    Health, beauty, vigour now decline,
The pride of Summer's splendid day,
    Leaves, which the stem must now resign,
The mournful prelude of decay.

    But let fair Virtue's fruit remain,
Through Summer with my leaves be fled;
    Then, not despised, I'll not complain,
But cherish Autumn in her stead.

by Anon.

Fall, Leaves, Fall

Fall, leaves, fall; die, flowers, away;

Lengthen night and **shorten day;**

Every leaf speaks BLISS to me

Fluttering from the autumn tree.

I shall smile when wreaths of snow

Blossom where the rose should grow;

I shall sing when night's ***DECAY***

Ushers in a **DREARIER DAY.**

by Emily Brontë

The Blind Boy

O say what is that thing called light,
Which I must ne'er enjoy?
What is the blessing of the sight?
O tell your poor blind boy!

You talk of wond'rous things you see,
You say the sun shines bright!
I feel him warm, but how can he
Then make it day or night?

My day or night myself I make,
Whene'er I wake or play;
And could I ever keep awake,
It would be always day.

With heavy sighs I often hear
You mourn my hopeless woe.
But sure with patience I may bear
A loss I ne'er can know.

Then let not what I cannot have
My cheer of mind destroy.
Whilst thus I sing, I am a king,
Although a poor blind boy!

by Colley Cibber

I Was Made Erect and Lone

I was made erect and lone
And within me is the bone
Still my vision will be clear
Still my life will not be drear
To the center all is near
Where I sit there is my throne
If age choose to sit apart
If age choose give me the start
Take the sap and leave the heart.

by Henry David Thoreau

First Fig

My candle burns at both ends;

It will not last the night;

But ah, my foes, and oh, my friends—

It gives a lovely light!

by Edna St Vincent Millay

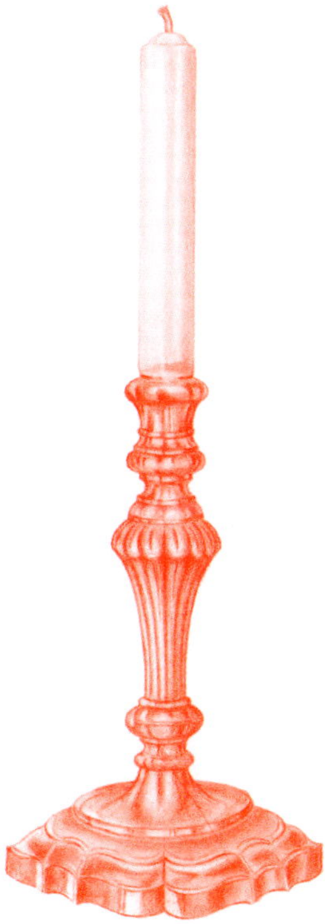

Space

Space, of course, is alive

that's why it moves about;

and that's what makes it eternally spacious and unstuffy.

And somewhere it has a WILD HEART
that sends pulses even through me;
and I call it the sun;
and I feel aristocratic, noble, when I feel a PULSE go through me
from the wild heart of space, that I call the SUN OF SUNS.

by D. H. Lawrence

Rubric

I'll not believe the dullard dark,
    Nor all the winds that weep,
But I shall find the farthest dream
    That kisses me, asleep.

by Josephine Preston Peabody

CHAPTER FIVE

Find Hope in the Everyday

"Making a green place in the city"

Time's Other Country
Michael Roberts

But First Make Tea

Five good morning posts

GOOD MORNING – Today is a day they hath named Nowday. Now is a perfect time to step into your future self in present form, but first some long think and many tasks that will test endurance and spirit and mettle, but first make tea.

GOOD MORNING – It is another day. Take one day at a time. One page at a time. Try to remember to use more guts stuff and heart stuff not always just the head stuff. Give the overthinks a rest today. The past is here and so is thy future, we meet in the present, but first make tea.

GOOD MORNING – For a moment just imagine having a lifetime of sunrises all in the same morning, how intense that would be, you think you want it all, but one sunrise per day is quite enough, do one job well at a time, rise and shine, but first make tea.

GOOD MORNING – Waking up hungry in this dark morning of the human, maybe porridge is the answer or justice or spring, probably all three, but first make tea.

GOOD MORNING – Time is liquid. Notice how each moment pours into the next. Swim into it. You're made of water and light. Your tides grow strong each day, look at you, you really are as miraculous as a fish, take a deep dive into new waters, but first make tea.

by Salena Godden

The Humdrum Way

When something unusual has to be done,
a perilous hill to be scaled,
a bridge to be crossed, a venture begun,
we think not of those who have failed,
but we tackle the job with courage and zest,
for really and truly it's fun
to feel that our strength is standing the test
when there's something of worth to be done.

When we feel we are watched by critical eyes,
when we know there's reward if we win,
it's neither a matter for praise nor surprise
that we're only too glad to begin;
for it's human to like the cheers and applause
that follow spectacular feats,
but save a few cheers for this other cause—
for the heroes in quiet little streets.

When the same old thing has got to be done—
a drab little, quiet little, everyday task,
a floor to be swept, a ledger begun,
then this is the boon we justly may ask—
that we may be given the strength, day by day,
to walk with sweet grace the dull, Humdrum Way.

by Wilhelmina Stitch

Time's Other Country

I walked, frowning, across the Cathedral Square,
I was late, and I had another appointment later,
The city crowded upon me, the walls narrowed;
And suddenly traffic, walls, loudspeakers vanished.

I have only to stop hurrying, and a seed springs up
Making a green place in the city, sweeping away the clock,
Fountains burst up through pavements hard as habit
Lightly I walk through a wall, and the sky is open.

Here again is truth, and infinite honesty,
The long unhurried diligence of childhood,
Measuring the exact length of a shadow, or chasing butterflies,
With the house dead quiet, and only a blackbird in the garden.

Out of the traffic, out of the tinkling glass,
There comes the apocalyptic galloping of horses;
I have seen the still water, like the eyes of heroes,
Here, on the other side of the wall, within six inches.

by Michael Roberts

All Nature Has a Feeling

All nature has a feeling: woods, fields, brooks
Are life eternal: and in silence they
Speak happiness beyond the reach of books;
There's nothing mortal in them; their decay
Is the green life of change; to pass away
And come again in blooms revivified.
Its birth was heaven, eternal is its stay,
And with the sun and moon shall still abide
Beneath their day and night and heaven wide.

by John Clare

Ode on a Distant Prospect of Eton College *(extract)*

Ye distant spires, ye antique towers,
That crown the watery glade,
Where grateful Science still adores
Her Henry's holy Shade;
And ye that from the stately brow
Of Windsor's heights the expanse below
Of grove, of lawn, of mead survey,
Whose turf, whose shade, whose flowers among
Wanders the hoary Thames along
His silver-winding way.

Ah, happy hills, ah, pleasing shade,
Ah, fields beloved in vain,
Where once my careless childhood strayed,
A stranger yet to pain!
I feel the gales, that from ye blow,
A momentary bliss bestow,
As waving fresh their gladsome wing,
My weary soul they seem to soothe,
And, redolent of joy and youth,
To breathe a second spring.

by Thomas Gray

Lochan *for Jean Johnstone*

When all this is over I mean
to travel north, by the high

drove roads and cart tracks
probably in June,

with the gentle dog-roses
flourishing beside me. I mean

to find among the thousands
scattered in that land

a certain quiet lochan,
where water lilies rise

like small fat moons,
and tied among the reeds,

underneath a rowan,
a white boat waits.

by Kathleen Jamie

The Storm

I ran to the forest for shelter
Breathless, half sobbing
I put my arms round a tree
Pillowed my head against the ***ROUGH BARK***

Protect me, I said. I am a LOST CHILD.
But the tree showered silver drops on my face and hair.
A wind sprang up from the ends of the earth

It ***LASHED*** the forest together
A huge green wave burst and thundered over my head.
I prayed, implored, *'Please take care of me.'*

But the wind pulled at my cloak and the ***RAIN BEAT UPON ME.***
Little rivers tore up the ground and swamped the bushes.
A ***FRENZY*** possessed the earth: I felt that the earth was drowning

In a bubbling cavern of s p a c e. I alone —
SMALLER THAN THE SMALLEST FLY — was alive and terrified.

Then, for what reason I know not, I became triumphant.
Well, kill me — *I cried* — and ran out into the open.

But the storm ceased: the sun spread his wings
And floated serene in the silver pool of the sky.

I put my hands over my face: *I was blushing*
And the trees swung together and DELICATELY LAUGHED.

by Katherine Mansfield

Endymion *(extract)*

A thing of beauty is a joy for ever:
Its loveliness increases; it will never
Pass into nothingness; but still will keep
A bower quiet for us, and a sleep
Full of sweet dreams, and health, and quiet breathing.
Therefore, on every morrow, are we wreathing
A flowery band to bind us to the earth,
Spite of despondence, of the inhuman dearth
Of noble natures, of the gloomy days,
Of all the unhealthy and o'er-darkened ways
Made for our searching: yes, in spite of all,
Some shape of beauty moves away the pall
From our dark spirits. Such the sun, the moon,
Trees old and young, sprouting a shady boon
For simple sheep; and such are daffodils
With the green world they live in; and clear rills
That for themselves a cooling covert make
'Gainst the hot season; the mid forest brake,
Rich with a sprinkling of fair musk-rose blooms.

by John Keats

Inscription for the Entrance to a Wood

Stranger, if thou hast learned a truth which needs
No school of long experience, that the world
Is full of guilt and misery, and hast seen
Enough of all its sorrows, crimes, and cares,
To tire thee of it, enter this wild wood
And view the haunts of Nature. The calm shade
Shall bring a kindred calm, and the sweet breeze
That makes the green leaves dance, shall waft a balm
To thy sick heart. Thou wilt find nothing here
Of all that pained thee in the haunts of men
And made thee loathe thy life. The primal curse
Fell, it is true, upon the unsinning earth,
But not in vengeance. God hath yoked to guilt
Her pale tormentor, misery. Hence, these shades
Are still the abodes of gladness; the thick roof
Of green and stirring branches is alive
And musical with birds, that sing and sport
In wantonness of spirit; while below
The squirrel, with raised paws and form erect,
Chirps merrily. Throngs of insects in the shade
Try their thin wings and dance in the warm beam
That waked them into life. Even the green trees
Partake the deep contentment; as they bend
To the soft winds, the sun from the blue sky
Looks in and sheds a blessing on the scene.

Scarce less the cleft-born wild-flower seems to enjoy
Existence, than the winged plunderer
That sucks its sweets. The massy rocks themselves,
And the old and ponderous trunks of prostrate trees
That lead from knoll to knoll a causey rude
Or bridge the sunken brook, and their dark roots,
With all their earth upon them, twisting high,
Breathe fixed tranquillity. The rivulet
Sends forth glad sounds, and tripping o'er its bed
Of pebbly sands, or leaping down the rocks,
Seems, with continuous laughter, to rejoice
In its own being. Softly tread the marge,
Lest from her midway perch thou scare the wren
That dips her bill in water. The cool wind,
That stirs the stream in play, shall come to thee,
Like one that loves thee nor will let thee pass
Ungreeted, and shall give its light embrace.

by William Cullen Bryant

The Heart of the Wood

My hope and my love,
we will go for a while into the wood,
scattering the dew,
where we will see the trout,
we will see the blackbird on its nest;
the deer and the buck calling,
the little bird that is sweetest singing on the branches;
the cuckoo on the top of the fresh green;
and death will never come near us
for ever in the sweet wood.

by Anon.
(translated by Lady Augusta Gregory)

Deep in the Quiet Wood

Are you bowed down in heart?
Do you but hear the clashing discords and the din of life?
Then come away, come to the peaceful wood.
Here bathe your soul in silence. Listen! Now,
From out the palpitating solitude
Do you not catch, yet faint, elusive strains?
They are above, around, within you, everywhere.
Silently listen! Clear, and still more clear, they come.
They bubble up in rippling notes, and swell in singing tones.
Now let your soul run the whole gamut of the wondrous scale
Until, responsive to the tonic chord,
It touches the diapason of God's grand cathedral organ,
Filling earth for you with heavenly peace
And holy harmonies.

by James Weldon Johnson

The Peace of Wild Things

When despair for the world **GROWS** in me
and I wake in the night at the least sound
in **FEAR** of what my life and my children's lives may be,
I go and lie down where the wood drake
rests in his *beauty* on the water, and the great heron feeds.
I come into the *peace* of wild things
who do not tax their lives with forethought
of grief. I come into the presence of *still water.*
And I feel above me the day-blind stars
waiting with their light. For a time
I rest in the *grace* of the world, and am *free*.

by Wendell Berry

Hope

O thrush, is it true?
Your song tells
Of a world born anew,
Of fields gold with buttercups, woodlands all blue
With hyacinth bells;
Of primroses deep
In the moss of the lane,
Of a Princess asleep
And dear magic to do.
Will the sun wake the princess? O thrush, is it true?
Will Spring come again?

Will Spring come again?
Now at last
With soft shine and rain
Will the violet be sweet where the dead leaves have lain?
Will Winter be past?
In the brown of the copse
Will white wind-flowers star through
Where the last oak-leaf drops?
Will the daisies come too,
And the may and the lilac? Will Spring come again?
O thrush, is it true?

by Edith Nesbit

The Unknown Bird

Three lovely notes he whistled, too soft to be heard
If others sang; but others never sang
In the great beech-wood all that May and June.
No one saw him: I alone could hear him:
Though many listened. Was it but four years
Ago? or five? He never came again.

Oftenest when I heard him I was alone,
Nor could I ever make another hear.
La-la-la! he called, seeming far-off – As if a cock
crowed past the edge of the world,
As if the bird or I were in a dream.
Yet that he travelled through the trees and sometimes
Neared me, was plain, though somehow distant still
He sounded. All the proof is – I told men
What I had heard.

I never knew a voice,
Man, beast, or bird, better than this. I told
The naturalists; but neither had they heard
Anything like the notes that did so haunt me,
I had them clear by heart and have them still.
Four years, or five, have made no difference. Then
As now that La-la-la! was bodiless sweet:
Sad more than joyful it was, if I must say
That it was one or other, but if sad

’Twas sad only with joy too, too far off
For me to taste it. But I cannot tell
If truly never anything but fair
The days were when he sang, as now they seem.
This surely I know, that I who listened then,
Happy sometimes, sometimes suffering
A heavy body and a heavy heart,
Now straightway, if I think of it, become
Light as that bird wandering beyond my shore.

by Edward Thomas

Proud Songsters

The thrushes sing as the sun is going,
And the finches whistle in ones and pairs,
And as it gets dark loud nightingales
    In bushes
Pipe, as they can when April wears,
    As if all Time were theirs.

These are brand-new birds of twelve-months' growing,
Which a year ago, or less than twain,
No finches were, nor nightingales,
    Nor thrushes,
But only particles of grain,
    And earth, and air, and rain.

by Thomas Hardy

The Sparrow

A little bird, with plumage brown,
Beside my window flutters down,
A moment chirps its little strain,
Ten taps upon my window-pane,
And chirps again, and hops along,
To call my notice to its song;
But I work on, nor heed its lay,
Till, in neglect, it flies away.

So birds of peace and hope and love
Come fluttering earthward from above,
To settle on life's window-sills,
And ease our load of earthly ills;
But we, in traffic's rush and din
Too deep engaged to let them in,
With deadened heart and sense plod on,
Nor know our loss till they are gone.

by Paul Laurence Dunbar

From Life and Death (Echoes)

The nightingale has a lyre of gold,
The lark's is a clarion-call,
And the blackbird plays but a box-wood flute,
But I love him best of all.

For his song is all of the joy of life,
And we in the mad, spring weather,
We two have listened till he sang
Our hearts and lips together.

by W. E. Henley

Meadowlarks

In the silver light after a storm,
Under dripping boughs of bright new green,
I take the low path to hear the meadowlarks
Alone and high-hearted as if I were a queen.

What have I to fear in life or death
Who have known three things: the kiss in the night,
The white flying joy when a song is born,
And meadowlarks whistling in silver light.

by Sara Teasdale

In the Fields

Lord when I look at lovely things which pass,
Under old trees the shadow of young leaves
Dancing to please the wind along the grass,
Or the gold stillness of the August sun on the August sheaves;
Can I believe there is a heavenlier world than this?
And if there is
Will the heart of any everlasting thing
Bring me these dreams that take my breath away?
They come at evening with the home-flying rooks and the scent
of hay,
Over the fields. They come in spring.

by Charlotte Mew

Kinnoull Hill

We sat on the verge of the steep
In a coign where the east wind failed.
In heaven's top, cradled, asleep,
The young sun basked, and deep
Into space the universe sailed.

And eastward the cliff rose higher,
And westward it sloped to the town,
That smoked like a smouldering fire
Built close about spire after spire;
And the smoke was pale-blue and brown.

The smell of the turf and the pine
Wound home to our heart's warm core;
And we knew by a secret sign
That earth is your mother and mine;
And we loved each other the more.

And out of the rock, scarred and bare,
The daws came crying in crowds,
And tossed themselves into the air,
And flew up and down, here and there.
And cast flying shadows, like clouds.

We heard not the lark, but we heard
The mellow, ineffable tune
Of a sweet-piping, wood-haunting bird.
Our heart-strings were stricken and stirred,
And we two were happy that noon.

by John Davidson

The Darkling Thrush

I leant upon a coppice gate
When Frost was spectre-grey,
And Winter's dregs made desolate
The weakening eye of day.
The tangled bine-stems scored the sky
Like strings of broken lyres,
And all mankind that haunted nigh
Had sought their household fires.

The land's sharp features seemed to be
The Century's corpse outleant,
His crypt the cloudy canopy,
The wind his death-lament.
The ancient pulse of germ and birth
Was shrunken hard and dry,
And every spirit upon earth
Seemed fervourless as I.

At once a voice arose among
The bleak twigs overhead
In a full-hearted evensong
Of joy illimited;
An aged thrush, frail, gaunt, and small,
In blast-beruffled plume,
Had chosen thus to fling his soul
Upon the growing gloom.

So little cause for carolings
    Of such ecstatic sound
Was written on terrestrial things
    Afar or nigh around,
That I could think there trembled through
    His happy good-night air
Some blessed Hope, whereof he knew
    And I was unaware.

by Thomas Hardy

Winter Bird

My bird, my darling,
Calling through the cold of afternoon –
Those round, bright notes,
Each one so perfect
Shaken from the other and yet
Hanging together in flashing clusters!
'The small soft flowers and the ripe fruit
All are gathered.
It is the season now of nuts and berries
And round, bright, flashing drops
In the frozen grass.'

by Katherine Mansfield

Emmonsail's Heath in Winter

I love to see the old heath's withered brake
Mingle its crimpled leaves with furze and ling,
While the old heron from the lonely lake
Starts slow and flaps his melancholy wing,
And oddling crow in idle motions swing
On the half-rotten ash-tree's topmost twig,
Beside whose trunk the gypsy makes his bed.
Up flies the bouncing woodcock from the brig
Where a black quagmire quakes beneath the tread;
The fieldfares chatter in the whistling thorn
And for the haw round fields and closen rove,
And coy bumbarrels, twenty in a drove,
Flit down the hedgerows in the frozen plain
And hang on little twigs and start again.

by John Clare

I Heard a Bird Sing

I heard a bird sing
In the dark of December
A magical thing
And sweet to remember.

'We are nearer to spring
Than we were in September,'
I heard a bird sing
In the dark of December.

by Oliver Herford

Pack, Clouds, Away, and Welcome Day

Pack, clouds, away, and welcome day,
    With night we banish sorrow;
Sweet air blow soft, mount larks aloft
    To give my Love good-morrow!
Wings from the wind to please her mind
    Notes from the lark I'll borrow;
Bird, prune thy wing, nightingale sing,
    To give my Love good-morrow;
        To give my Love good-morrow
        Notes from them both I'll borrow.

Wake from thy nest, Robin-red-breast,
    Sing, birds, in every furrow;
And from each hill, let music shrill
    Give my fair Love good-morrow!
Blackbird and thrush in every bush,
    Stare, linnet, and cock-sparrow!
You pretty elves, amongst yourselves
    Sing my fair Love good-morrow;
        To give my Love good-morrow
        Sing, birds, in every furrow!

by Thomas Heywood

The Ailanthus Tree

She has a few leaves left to see by;
her straggling boughs
can no longer hide from the tenement windows
the ailanthus tree that is going blind so young.
Swarming with sparrows,
she squats like a beggar at the back doors
and rocks in the wind
that sidles to her through the clothes-lines.
But at the least glance of the sun –
swaggering provocatively over high roofs –
the leaves, waxen-green, that play precariously at the ends of high twigs,
light up shyly ... and with an eager glisten.

by Lola Ridge

Pippa's Song

The year's at the spring,
And day's at the morn;
Morning's at seven;
The hill-side's dew-pearl'd;
The lark's on the wing;
The snail's on the thorn;
God's in His heaven –
All's right with the world!

by Robert Browning

Now the Noisy Winds Are Still

Now the noisy winds are still;

April's coming up the hill!

All the spring is in her train,

Led by shining ranks of rain;

Pit, pat, patter, clatter,

Sudden sun, and *clatter, patter!—*

First the blue, and then the SHOWER;

Bursting bud, and *smiling flower;*

Brooks set free with *tinkling ring;*

Birds too full of song to sing;

Crisp old leaves *astir with pride,*

Where the timid violets hide—

All things ready *with a will—*

April's coming up the hill!

by Mary Mapes Dodge

An April Day

On such a day as this I think,
  On such as day as this,
When earth and sky and nature's whole
  Are clad in April's bliss;
And balmy zephyrs gently waft
  Upon your cheek a kiss;
Sufficient is it just to live
  On such a day as this.

by Joseph Seamon Cotter Jr.

Sonnet

I had not thought of violets late,
The wild, shy kind that spring beneath your feet
In wistful April days, when lovers mate
And wander through the fields in raptures sweet.
The thought of violets meant florists' shops,
And bows and pins, and perfumed papers fine;
And garish lights, and mincing little fops
And cabarets and soaps, and deadening wines.
So far from sweet real things my thoughts had strayed,
I had forgot wide fields; and clear brown streams;
The perfect loveliness that God has made,—
Wild violets shy and Heaven-mounting dreams.
And now—unwittingly, you've made me dream
Of violets, and my soul's forgotten gleam.

by Alice Dunbar Nelson

The Argument of His Book

I sing of brooks, of blossoms, birds, and bowers,
Of April, May, of June, and July flowers;
I sing of may-poles, hock-carts, wassails, wakes,
Of bridegrooms, brides, and of their bridal cakes;
I write of youth, of love, and have access
By these to sing of cleanly wantonness;
I sing of dews, of rains, and piece by piece
Of balm, of oil, of spice, and ambergris;
I sing of times trans-shifting, and I write
How roses first came red, and lilies white;
I write of groves, of twilights, and I sing
The court of Mab, and of the Fairy King;
I write of hell; I sing, and ever shall,
Of heaven, and hope to have it after all.

by Robert Herrick

The Hymn of Empedocles *(extract)*

Is it so small a thing
    To have enjoy'd the sun,
    To have lived light in the spring,
    To have loved, to have thought, to have done;
To have advanced true friends, and beat down baffling foes;

by Matthew Arnold

Mist

Low-anchored cloud,

Newfoundland air,

Fountain-head and source of rivers,

Dew-cloth, dream-drapery,

And napkin spread by fays;

Drifting meadow of the air,

Where bloom the daisied banks and violets,

And in whose fenny labyrinth

The bittern booms and heron wades;

Spirit of lakes and seas and rivers,—

Bear only perfumes and the scent

Of healing herbs to just men's fields.

by Henry David Thoreau

A Fine Day

After all the rain, the sun
Shines on hill and grassy mead;
Fly into the garden, child,
You are very glad indeed.

For the days have been so dull,
Oh, so special dark and drear,
That you told me, 'Mr Sun
Has forgotten we live here.'

Dew upon the lily lawn,
Dew upon the garden beds;
Daintily from all the leaves
Pop the little primrose heads.

And the violets in the copse
With their parasols of green
Take a little peek at you;
They're the bluest you have seen.

On the lilac tree a bird
Singing first a little note,
Then a burst of happy song
Bubbles in his lifted throat.

O the sun, the comfy sun!
This the song that you must sing,
'Thank you for the birds, the flowers,
Thank you, sun, for everything.'

by Katherine Mansfield

Pause

When I am very earnestly digging
I lift my head sometimes, and look at the mountains,
And muse upon them, muscles relaxing

I think how freely the wild grasses flower there,
How grandly the storm-shaped trees are massed in their gorges,
And the rain-worn rocks strewn in magnificent heaps,

Pioneer plants on those uplands find their own footings
No vigorous growth, there, is an evil weed:
All weathers are salutary.

It is only a little while since this hillside
Lay untrammelled likewise,
Unceasingly swept by transmarine winds.

In a very little while, it may be,
When our impulsive limbs and our superior skulls
Have to the soil restored several ounces of fertiliser,

The Mother of all will take charge again,
And soon wipe away with her elements
Our small fond human enclosures.

by Ursula Bethell

Only Some Spires

Only some spires of bright green grass
Transparently in sunshine quivering.

by Emily Brontë

The Sower

Sitting in a porchway cool,
Sunlight, I see, dying fast,
Twilight hastens on to rule.
Working hours have well-nigh past.
Shadows run across the lands:
But a sower lingers still,
Old, in rags, he patient stands.
Looking on, I feel a thrill.
Black and high, his silhouette
Dominates the furrows deep!
Now to sow the task is set.
Soon shall come a time to reap.
Marches he along the plain
To and fro, and scatters wide
From his hands the precious grain;
Muse I, as I see him stride.
Darkness deepens. Fades the light.
Now his gestures to mine eyes
Are august; and strange, - his height
Seems to touch the starry skies

by Toru Dutt

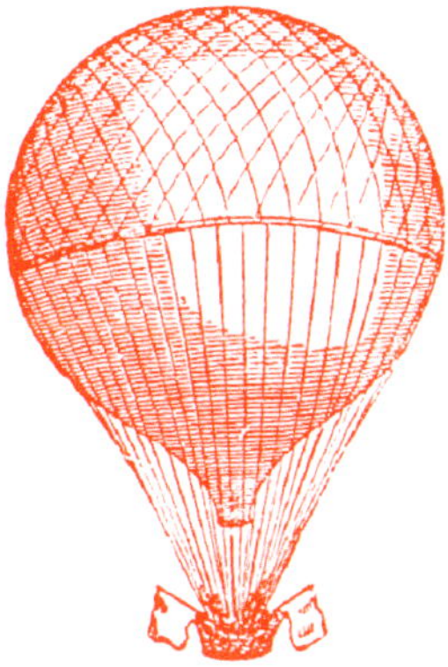

My Soul is Awakened, My Spirit is Soaring

My soul is awakened, my spirit is soaring,
And carried aloft on the wings of the breeze;
For, above, and around me, the wild wind is roaring
Arousing to rapture the earth and the seas.

The long withered grass in the sunshine is glancing,
The bare trees are tossing their branches on high;
The dead leaves beneath them are merrily dancing,
The white clouds are scudding across the blue sky.

I wish I could see how the ocean is lashing
The foam of its billows to whirlwinds of spray,
I wish I could see how its proud waves are dashing
And hear the wild roar of their thunder today!

by Anne Brontë

Reciprocity

I do not think that skies and meadows are
Moral, or that the fixture of a star
Comes of a quiet spirit, or that trees
Have wisdom in their windless silences.
Yet these are things invested in my mood
With constancy, and peace, and fortitude,
That in my troubled season I can cry
Upon the wide composure of the sky,
And envy fields, and wish that I might be
As little daunted as a star or tree.

by John Drinkwater

Speak of the North!

Speak of the North! A lonely moor
Silent and dark and trackless swells,
The waves of some wild streamlet pour
Hurriedly through its ferny dells.

Profoundly still the twilight air,
Lifeless the landscape; so we deem,
Till like a phantom gliding near
A stag bends down to drink the stream.

And far away a mountain zone,
A cold, white waste of snow-drifts lies,
And one star, large and soft and lone,
Silently lights the unclouded skies.

by Charlotte Brontë

In the Train

Fields beneath a quilt of snow
    From which the rocks and stubble peep,
And in the west a shy white star
    That shivers as it wakes from sleep.
The restless rumble of the train,
    The drowsy people in the car,
Steel blue twilight in the world,
    And in my heart a timid star.

by Sara Teasdale

Miracles

Why, who makes much of a miracle?
As to me I know of nothing else but miracles,
Whether I walk the streets of Manhattan,
Or dart my sight over the roofs of houses toward the sky,
Or wade with naked feet along the beach just in the edge of the water,
Or stand under trees in the woods,
Or talk by day with any one I love, or sleep in the bed at night with
any one I love,
Or sit at table at dinner with the rest,
Or look at strangers opposite me riding in the car,
Or watch honey-bees busy around the hive of a summer forenoon,
Or animals feeding in the fields,
Or birds, or the wonderfulness of insects in the air,
Or the wonderfulness of the sundown, or of stars shining so quiet
and bright,
Or the exquisite delicate thin curve of the new moon in spring;
These with the rest, one and all, are to me miracles,
The whole referring, yet each distinct and in its place.
To me every hour of the light and dark is a miracle,
Every cubic inch of space is a miracle,
Every square yard of the surface of the earth is spread with the same,
Every foot of the interior swarms with the same.

To me the sea is a continual miracle,
The fishes that swim – the rocks – the motion of the waves –
the ships with men in them,
What stranger miracles are there?

by Walt Whitman

Desiderata

Go placidly amid the noise and the haste, and remember what peace there may be in silence. As far as possible without surrender be on good terms with all persons.

Speak your truth quietly and clearly; and listen to others, even to the dull and the ignorant, they too have their story. Avoid loud and aggressive persons, they are vexations to the spirit.

If you compare yourself to others, you may become vain and bitter; for always there will be greater and lesser persons than yourself.

Enjoy your achievements as well as your plans. Keep interested in your own career, however humble; it is a real possession in the changing fortunes of time.

Exercise caution in your business affairs, for the world is full of trickery. But let not this blind you to what virtue there is; many persons strive for high ideals, and everywhere life is full of heroism.

Be yourself. Especially do not feign affection. Neither be cynical about love; for in the face of all aridity and disenchantment it is as perennial as the grass. Take kindly the counsel of the years, gracefully surrendering the things of youth.

Nurture strength of spirit to shield you in sudden misfortune. But do not distress yourself with dark imaginings. Many fears are born of fatigue and loneliness.

Beyond a wholesome discipline, be gentle with yourself. You are a child of the universe, no less than the trees and the stars; you have a right to be here. And whether or not it is clear to you, no doubt the universe is unfolding as it should.

Therefore, be at peace with God, whatever you conceive him to be, and whatever your labours and aspirations in the noisy confusion of life, keep peace in your soul. With all its sham, drudgery and broken dreams, it is still a beautiful world.

Be cheerful. Strive to be happy.

by Max Ehrmann

CHAPTER SIX

A New Dawn

"Take heart with the day and begin again"

New Every Morning
Susan Coolidge

Morning Sleep *(extract)*

Another day hath dawned
Since, hastily and tired, I threw myself
Into the dark lap of advancing sleep.
Meanwhile through the oblivion of the night
The ponderous world its old course hath fulfilled;
And now the gradual sun begins to throw
Its slanting glory on the heads of trees,
And every bird stirs in its nest revealed,
And shakes its dewy wings.

by William Bell Scott

New Every Morning

Every day is a fresh beginning,
Listen my soul to the glad refrain.
And, spite of old sorrows
And older sinning,
Troubles forecasted
And possible pain,
Take heart with the day and begin again.

by Susan Coolidge

Today and Tomorrow

TODAY

Unsullied comes to thee, new-born;
Tomorrow is not thine.
The sun may cease to shine
For thee ere earth shall greet its morn.
Be earnest then, in thought and deed,
Nor fear approaching night;
Calm comes with evening light,
And hope and peace. Thy duty heed
TODAY.

by John Ruskin

Look Forward

What a mess I made of things! That was yesterday.
Yesterday has taken wings—Hide mistakes away.

Things I did can't be undone. Silly then to sorrow.
Better is the task begun on a bright new morrow.

If I hadn't acted thus! Silence, puling heart.
Useless now to fume and fuss, make a brand new start.

All the energy that goes into senseless fretting
Would rebuild, if you so chose, your plan in some new setting.

What a blow! Fate is unkind. Grit your teeth, don't murmur.
Smile as if you didn't mind, stand a little firmer.

Here is solace for your grief, nothing's done beyond recall.
Smudged a page? Well, turn a leaf. Begin again. That's all.

Failed to-day? To-day is past. To-morrow's peeping round the door.
Never doubt you'll win at last. That is what to-morrow's for.

by Wilhelmina Stitch

Jack the Giant Queller *(extract)*

Arise, arise, arise!
Each shape, and sort, and size
Of honesty, where ye lie
Unheeded, on dank or dry,
From cottages, sheds and steads, to court,
My brothers of worth and want, resort;
Arise to labour, arise to play,
For Virtue dawns, a newborn day.

by Henry Brooke

Invocation

As pools beneath stone arches take
Darkly within their deeps again
Shapes of the flowing stone, and make
Stories anew of passing men,

So let the living thoughts that keep,
Morning and evening, in their kind,
Eternal change in height and deep,
Be mirrored in my happy mind.

Beat, world, upon this heart, be loud
Your marvel chanted in my blood.
Come forth, O sun, through cloud on cloud
To shine upon my stubborn mood.

Great hills that fold above the sea,
Ecstatic airs and sparkling skies,
Sing out your words to master me—
Make me immoderately wise.

by John Drinkwater

Resolution and Independence *(extract)*

There was a roaring in the wind all night;
The rain came heavily and fell in floods;
But now the sun is rising calm and bright;
The birds are singing in the distant woods;
Over his own sweet voice the stock-dove broods;
The jay makes answer as the magpie chatters;
And all the air is filled with pleasant noise of waters.

All things that love the sun are out of doors;
The sky rejoices in the morning's birth;
The grass is bright with rain-drops;—on the moors
The hare is running races in her mirth;
And with her feet she from the plashy earth
Raises a mist; that, glittering in the sun,
Runs with her all the way, wherever she doth run.

by William Wordsworth

Cymbeline, Act II, Scene III *(extract)*

Hark, hark, the lark at heaven's gate sings,
And Phoebus 'gins arise,
His steeds to water at those springs
On chaliced flowers that lies;
And winking Mary-buds begin to ope their golden eyes:
With every thing that pretty is, my lady sweet, arise:
Arise, arise!

by William Shakespeare

Tomorrow

Tomorrow, there will be enough
of food, and warmth and love, and hope.

Tomorrow, the birds WILL sing.

Tomorrow, fear and hate will be outlawed
and dreams, good dreams, will have a place
in everybody's lives.

Tomorrow, the birds WILL sing.

Tomorrow, there will be no more calls to arms, to war.
No more pitting soul against soul
until even the bravest dies a little inside.

Tomorrow, the birds WILL sing.

Tomorrow, you will see there is
a reason to go on,
a light that shines,
a field that beckons –
in truth, there will be all you ever hoped for.
You will walk in peace
in the green field, under the sun
that warms, that mends.

Until then, take heart, friend
and be glad you live.
Touch each life you meet
with your own truth
and with this just and certain hope –

Tomorrow, the birds WILL sing.
For each, for everyone.

by Helen Burke

Stray Birds *(extract)*

205

When the sun goes down to the West, the East of his morning stands before him in silence.

by Rabindranath Tagore

Hear the Voice of the Bard

Hear the voice of the Bard!
Who present, past, and future sees;
Whose ears have heard
The Holy Word
That walked among the ancient trees,

Calling the lapsèd soul,
And weeping in the evening dew;
That might control
The starry pole,
And fallen, fallen light renew!

'O Earth, O Earth, return!
Arise from out the dewy grass;
Night is worn,
And the morn
Rises from the slumbrous mass.

Turn away no more;
Why wilt thou turn away?
The starry floor,
The watery shore,
Is given thee till the break of day.'

by William Blake

Living

Slow bleak awakening from the morning dream
Brings me in contact with the sudden day.
I am alive – this I.
I let my fingers move along my body.
Realization warns them, and my nerves
Prepare their rapid messages and signals.
While Memory begins recording, coding,
Repeating; all the time Imagination
Mutters: You'll only die.

Here's a new day. O Pendulum move slowly!
My usual clothes are waiting on their peg.
I am alive – this I.
And in a moment Habit, like a crane,
Will bow its neck and dip its pulleyed cable,
Gathering me, my body, and our garment,
And swing me forth, oblivious of my question,
Into the daylight – why?

I think of all the others who awaken,
And wonder if they go to meet the morning
More valiantly than I;
Nor asking of this Day they will be living:
What have I done that I should be alive?
O, can I not forget that I am living?
How shall I reconcile the two conditions:
Living, and yet – to die?

Between the curtains the autumnal sunlight
With lean and yellow finger points me out;
The clock moans: Why? Why? Why?
But suddenly, as if without a reason,
Heart, Brain, and Body, and Imagination
All gather in tumultuous joy together,
Running like children down the path of morning
To fields where they can play without a quarrel:
A country I'd forgotten, but remember,
And welcome with a cry.

O cool glad pasture; living tree, tall corn,
Great cliff, or languid sloping sand, cold sea,
Waves; rivers curving; you, eternal flowers,
Give me content, while I can think of you:
Give me your living breath!
Back to your rampart, Death.

by Harold Munro

The Pillar of the Cloud

Lead kindly light amid the encircling gloom
Lead Thou me on!
The night is dark and I am far from home –
Lead Thou me on!
Keep Thou my feet: I do not ask to see
The distant scene, – one step enough for me.

I was not ever thus, nor pray'd that Thou
Shouldst lead me on.
I lov'd to choose and see my path; but now
Lead Thou me on!
I lov'd the garish day, and, spite of fears,
Pride ruled my will: remember not past years.

So long Thy power hath blest me, sure it still
Will lead me on,
O'er moor and fen, o'er crag and torrent, till
The night is gone;
And with the morn those angel faces smile
Which I have lov'd long since and lost awhile.

by John Henry Newman

Poem for a New Year

Something's moving in
I hear the weather in the wind
sense the tension of a sheep-field
and the pilgrimage of fins.

Something's not the same
I taste the sap and feel the grain
hear the rolling of the rowan
ringing, singing in a change.

Something's set to start
there's meadow-music in the dark
and the clouds that shroud the mountain
slowly, softly start to part.

by Matt Goodfellow

Passage to India *(extract)*

Year at whose wide-flung door I sing!
Year of the purpose accomplish'd!
Year of the marriage of continents, climates and oceans!
(No mere doge of Venice now wedding the Adriatic,)
I see, O year in you the vast terraqueous globe given and giving all,
Europe to Asia, Africa join'd, and they to the New World,
The lands, geographies, dancing before you, holding a festival garland,
As brides and bridegrooms hand in hand.

by Walt Whitman

The Burning of the Leaves

Now is the time for the burning of the leaves.
They go to the fire; the nostril pricks with smoke
Wandering slowly into a weeping mist.
Brittle and blotched, ragged and rotten sheaves!
A flame seizes the smouldering ruin and bites
On stubborn stalks that crackle as they resist.

The last hollyhock's fallen tower is dust;
All the spices of June are a bitter reek,
All the extravagant riches spent and mean.
All burns! The reddest rose is a ghost;
Sparks whirl up, to expire in the mist: the wild
Fingers of fire are making corruption clean.

Now is the time for stripping the spirit bare,
Time for the burning of days ended and done,
Idle solace of things that have gone before:
Rootless hope and fruitless desire are there;
Let them go to the fire, with never a look behind.
The world that was ours is a world that is ours no more.

They will come again, the leaf and the flower, to arise
From squalor of rottenness into the old splendour,
And magical scents to a wondering memory bring;
The same glory, to shine upon different eyes.
Earth cares for her own ruins, naught for ours.
Nothing is certain, only the certain spring.

by Laurence Binyon

Ceremony

Clear away the dead wood and feed the hungry fire
with every dragged branch, half-rotten log,
handful of leaves within your reach.

Twist and bend, dancing that ancient forgotten thing,
hands in gloves, sodden and chilling. Pause to drink
tea from the flask, eat Christmas cake, eat fast.

Then turn, catch cloudy breath just long enough
to see the clearing grow. Watch flames swallow
brushwood, breathe out tongues that shiver up to sky.

Work on until the fat moon rises low and calls time
on the day. Only now can you walk away,
into the cool dark, while fire burns out its heart.

You may return when charred ground is rain-soft,
pace the earth and count the space each tree
will need to thrive. Now dig the holes and plant.

by Helen Cadbury

Lycidas *(extract)*

Now, Lycidas, the shepherds weep no more;
Henceforth thou art the Genius of the shore,
In thy large recompense, and shalt be good
To all that wander in that perilous flood.

Thus sang the uncouth swain to the oaks and rills,
While the still morn went out with sandals grey;
He touched the tender stops of various quills,
With eager thought warbling his Doric lay.
And now the sun had stretched out all the hills,
And now was dropped into the western bay;
At last he rose, and twitched his mantle blue:
Tomorrow to fresh woods, and pastures new.

by John Milton

Ode to the West Wind *(extract)*

Make me thy lyre, even as the forest is:
What if my leaves are falling like its own?
The tumult of thy mighty harmonies

Will take from both a deep autumnal tone,
Sweet though in sadness. Be thou, Spirit fierce,
My spirit! Be thou me, impetuous one!

Drive my dead thoughts over the universe,
Like withered leaves, to quicken a new birth;
And, by the incantation of this verse,

Scatter, as from an unextinguished hearth
Ashes and sparks, my words among mankind!
Be through my lips to unawakened earth

The trumpet of a prophecy! O Wind,
If Winter comes, can Spring be far behind?

by Percy Bysshe Shelly

The Call

From our low seat beside the fire
Where we have dozed and dreamed and watched the glow
Or raked the ashes, stopping so
We scarcely saw the sun or rain
Above, or looked much higher
Than this same quiet red or burned-out fire.
To-night we heard a call,
A rattle on the window-pane,
A voice on the sharp air,
And felt a breath stirring our hair,
A flame within us: Something swift and tall
Swept in and out and that was all.
Was it a bright or a dark angel? Who can know?
It left no mark upon the snow,
But suddenly it snapped the chain
Unbarred, flung wide the door
Which will not shut again;
And so we cannot sit here any more.
We must arise and go:
The world is cold without
And dark and hedged about
With mystery and enmity and doubt,
But we must go
Though yet we do not know
Who called, or what marks we shall leave upon the snow.

by Charlotte Mew

Winter *(extract)*

I, singularly moved
To love the lovely that are not beloved,
Of all the Seasons, most
Love Winter, and to trace
The sense of the Trophonian pallor on her face.
It is not death, but plenitude of peace;
And the dim cloud that does the world enfold
Hath less the characters of dark and cold
Than warmth and light asleep,
And correspondent breathing seems to keep
With the infant harvest, breathing soft below
Its eider coverlet of snow.
Nor is in field or garden anything
But, duly looked into, contains serene
The substance of things hoped for, in the Spring,
And evidence of Summer not yet seen.

by Coventry Patmore

I Wandered Lonely as a Cloud

I wandered lonely as a cloud
That floats on high o'er vales and hills,
When all at once I saw a crowd,
A host, of golden daffodils;
Beside the lake, beneath the trees,
Fluttering and dancing in the breeze.

Continuous as the stars that shine
And twinkle on the milky way,
They stretched in never-ending line
Along the margin of a bay:
Ten thousand saw I at a glance,
Tossing their heads in sprightly dance.

The waves beside them danced; but they
Out-did the sparkling waves in glee:
A poet could not but be gay,
In such a jocund company:
I gazed – and gazed – but little thought
What wealth the show to me had brought:

For oft, when on my couch I lie
In vacant or in a pensive mood,
They flash upon that inward eye
Which is the bliss of solitude;
And then my heart with pleasure fills,
And dances with the daffodils.

by William Wordsworth

The Throstle

'Summer is coming, summer is coming.
    I know it, I know it, I know it.
Light again, leaf again, life again, love again,'
    Yes, my wild little Poet.

Sing the new year in under the blue.
    Last year you sang it as gladly.
'New, new, new, new'! Is it then *so* new
    That you should carol so madly?

'Love again, song again, nest again, young again,'
    Never a prophet so crazy!
And hardly a daisy as yet, little friend,
    See, there is hardly a daisy.

'Here again, here, here, here, happy year'!
    O warble unchidden, unbidden!
Summer is coming, is coming, my dear,
    And all the winters are hidden.

by Alfred, Lord Tennyson

Thaw

Over the land freckled with snow half-thawed
The speculating rooks at their nests cawed
And saw from elm-tops, delicate as flower of grass,
What we below could not see, Winter pass.

by Edward Thomas

Atalanta in Calydon *(extract)*

For winter's rains and ruins are over,
    And all the season of snows and sins;
The days dividing lover and lover,
    The light that loses, the night that wins;
And time remembered is grief forgotten,
And frosts are slain and flowers begotten,
And in green underwood and cover
    Blossom by blossom the spring begins.

by Algernon Charles Swinburne

In Memorium A. H. H. *(extract)*

Now fades the last long streak of snow,
Now burgeons every maze of quick
About the flowering squares, and thick
By ashen roots the violets blow.

Now rings the woodland loud and long,
The distance takes a lovelier hue,
And drown'd in yonder living blue
The lark becomes a sightless song.

Now dance the lights on lawn and lea,
The flocks are whiter down the vale,
And milkier every milky sail
On winding stream or distant sea;

Where now the seamew pipes, or dives
In yonder greening gleam, and fly
The happy birds, that change their sky
To build and brood; that live their lives

From land to land; and in my breast
Spring wakens too; and my regret
Becomes an April violet,
And buds and blossoms like the rest.

by Alfred Lord Tennyson

March

Now I know that Spring will come again,
Perhaps tomorrow: however late I've patience
After this night following on such a day.

While still my temples ached from the cold burning
Of hail and wind, and still the primroses
Torn by the hail were covered up in it,
The sun filled earth and heaven with a great light
And a tenderness, almost warmth, where the hail dripped,
As if the mighty sun wept tears of joy.
But 'twas too late for warmth. The sunset piled
Mountains on mountains of snow and ice in the west:
Somewhere among their folds the wind was lost,
And yet 'twas cold, and though I knew that Spring
Would come again, I knew it had not come,
That it was lost too in those mountains chill.

What did the thrushes know? Rain, snow, sleet, hail,
Had kept them quiet as the primroses.
They had but an hour to sing. On boughs they sang,
On gates, on ground; they sang while they changed perches
And while they fought, if they remembered to fight:
So earnest were they to pack into that hour
Their unwilling hoard of song before the moon
Grew brighter than the clouds. Then 'twas no time
For singing merely. So they could keep off silence
And night, they cared not what they sang or screamed;
Whether 'twas hoarse or sweet or fierce or soft;
And to me all was sweet: they could do no wrong.
Something they knew – I also, while they sang
And after. Not till night had half its stars
And never a cloud, was I aware of silence
Stained with all that hour's songs, a silence
Saying that Spring returns, perhaps tomorrow.

by Edward Thomas

The Rain

I hear leaves drinking rain;

I hear rich leaves on top

Giving the poor beneath

Drop after drop;

’Tis a sweet noise to hear

These green leaves drinking near.

And when the Sun comes out,

After this rain shall stop,

A wondrous light will fill

Each dark, round drop;

I hope the Sun shines bright;

’Twill be a lovely sight.

by W. H. Davies

After the Winter

Some day, when trees have shed their leaves
    And against the morning's white
The shivering birds beneath the eaves
    Have sheltered for the night,
We'll turn our faces southward, love,
    Toward the summer isle
Where bamboos spire the shafted grove
    And wide-mouthed orchids smile.

And we will seek the quiet hill
    Where towers the cotton tree,
And leaps the laughing crystal rill,
    And works the droning bee.
And we will build a cottage there
    Beside an open glade,
With black-ribbed blue-bells blowing near,
    And ferns that never fade.

by Claude McKay

An Instinct of Hope

Is there another world for this frail dust
To warm with life and be itself again?
Something about me daily speaks there must,
And why should instinct nourish hopes in vain?
'Tis nature's prophecy that such will be,
And everything seems struggling to explain
The close sealed volume of its mystery.
Time wandering onward keeps its usual pace
As seeming anxious of eternity,
To meet that calm and find a resting place.
E'en the small violet feels a future power
And waits each year renewing blooms to bring,
And surely man is no inferior flower
To die unworthy of a second spring?

by John Clare

The Coming of Good-Luck

So Good-Luck came, and on my roof did light,
Like noiseless snow, or as the dew of night;
Not all at once, but gently,—as the trees
Are by the sun-beams, tickled by degrees.

by Robert Herrick

Re-birth

Though your wild dreams
May die perhaps on the cemented stone
That they have cracked asunder ... making way
For lopped things trampled in the dust and blood
Of the year's barricades ... and hopes that died
Alone against blank walls ... yet what new growths
Against the cobbled ways ... and all the green
Battened down dreams of the world quickening ...
Like spirals of aborted pines that strain
To touch their tips with stars.

by Lola Ridge

The Trees

The trees are coming into leaf
Like something almost being said;
The recent buds relax and spread,
Their greenness is a kind of grief.

Is it that they are born again
And we grow old? No, they die too.
Their yearly trick of looking new
Is written down in rings of grain.

Yet still the unresting castles thresh
In fullgrown thickness every May.
Last year is dead, they seem to say,
Begin afresh, afresh, afresh.

by Philip Larkin

Spring Song

All winter through I sat alone,
Doors barred and windows shuttered fast,
And listened to the wind's faint moan,
And ghostly mutterings of the past;
And in the pauses of the rain,
'Mid whispers of dead sorrow and sin,
Love tapped upon the window pain:
I had no heart to let him in.

But now, with spring, my doors stand wide;
My windows let delight creep through;
I hear the skylark sing outside;
I see the crocus, golden new.
The pigeons on my window-sill,
Winging and wooing, flirt and flout –
Now Love must enter if he will,
I have no heart to keep him out.

by Edith Nesbit

Spring

Nothing is so beautiful as Spring –
    When weeds, in wheels, shoot long and lovely and lush;
    Thrush's eggs look little low heavens, and thrush
Through the echoing timber does so rinse and wring
The ear, it strikes like lightnings to hear him sing;
    The glassy peartree leaves and blooms, they brush
    The descending blue; that blue is all in a rush
With richness; the racing lambs too have fair their fling.

What is all this juice and all this joy?
    A strain of the earth's sweet being in the beginning
In Eden garden. – Have, get, before it cloy,
    Before it cloud, Christ, lord, and sour with sinning,
Innocent mind and Mayday in girl and boy,
    Most, O maid's child, thy choice and worthy the winning.

by Gerard Manley Hopkins

The Flower *(extract)*

How fresh, oh Lord, how sweet and clean
Are thy returns, even as the flowers in spring;
To which, besides their own demean,
The late-past frosts tributes of pleasure bring.
Grief melts away
Like snow in May,
As if there were no such cold thing.

by George Herbert

May, 1915

Let us remember Spring will come again
To the scorched blackened woods where all the wounded trees
Wait, with the old wise patience for the heavenly rain,
Sure of the sky, sure of the sea to send its healing breeze,
Sure of the sun. And even as to these
Surely the Spring, when God shall please
Will come again like a divine surprise
To those who sit to-day with their Great Dead, hands in their hands, eyes in their eyes,
At one with Love, at one with Grief, blind to the scattered things and changing skies.

by Charlotte Mew

There Will Come Soft Rains

There will come soft rains and the smell of the ground,
And swallows circling with their shimmering sound;

And frogs in the pools singing at night,
And wild plum trees in tremulous white;

Robins will wear their feathery fire,
Whistling their whims on a low fence-wire;

And not one will know of the war, not one
Will care at last when it is done.

Not one would mind, neither bird nor tree,
If mankind perished utterly;

And Spring herself, when she woke at dawn
Would scarcely know that we were gone.

by Sara Teasdale

Envoy

Go, songs, for ended is our brief, sweet play;
    Go, children of swift joy and tardy sorrow!
And some are sung, and that was yesterday,
    And some unsung, and that may be to-morrow.

Go forth; and if it be o'er stony way,
    Old joy can lend what newer grief must borrow:
And it was sweet, and that was yesterday,
    And sweet is sweet, though purchased with sorrow.

Go, songs, and come not back from your far way;
    And if men ask you why ye smile and sorrow,
Tell them ye grieve, for your hearts know To-day,
    Tell them ye smile, for your eyes know To-morrow.

by Francis Thompson

Ode on the Pleasure Arising from Vicissitude *(extract)*

Yesterday the sullen year
Saw the snowy whirlwind fly;
Mute was the music of the air,
The herd stood drooping by:
Their raptures now that wildly flow
No yesterday nor morrow know;
'Tis man alone that joy descries
With forward and reverted eyes.

Smiles on past Misfortune's brow
Soft Reflection's hand can trace;
And o'er the cheek of Sorrow throw
A melancholy grace;
While Hope prolongs our happier hour,
Or deepest shades, that dimly lour
And blacken round our weary way,
Gilds with a gleam of distant day.

Still, where rosy Pleasure leads,
See a kindred Grief pursue;
Behind the steps that Misery treads,
Approaching Comfort view:
The hues of bliss more brightly glow,
Chastised by sabler tints of woe;
And blended form, with artful strife,
The strength and harmony of life.

See the wretch, that long has tossed
On the thorny bed of pain,
At length repair his vigour lost,
And breathe and walk again:
The meanest flowret of the vale,
The simplest note that swells the gale,
The common sun, the air and skies,
To him are opening paradise.

by Thomas Gray

I Dwell in Possibility

I dwell in Possibility—
A fairer House than Prose—
More numerous of Windows—
Superior—for Doors—

Of Chambers as the Cedars—
Impregnable of Eye—
And for an Everlasting Roof
The Gambrels of the Sky—

Of Visitors—the fairest—
For Occupation—This—
The spreading wide my narrow Hands
To gather Paradise—

by Emily Dickinson

Hope *(extract)*

Tomorrow will be beautiful,
For tomorrow comes out of the lake.

by Emanuel Carnevali

First Day of Summer

What comforts me is that after
loss or love, the year still turns.
Nothing you or I can suffer
stops the May greens falling back
on time so June can have its day.
When I think it's over, the end
of everything, somehow there's always more,
and often it's more than I hoped for.

I know life takes, and takes. But look:
outside there are fields whose turn it is
to grow the crop, and others left
to lie quiet, and even in the fallow fields,
even in the muddiest, most godforsaken
fox-holes, the earth still wakes up
each morning and covers herself
with flowers.

by Rachel Jeffcoat

From a Window

Up here, with June, the sycamore throws
Across the window a whispering screen;
I shall miss the sycamore more, I suppose,
Than anything else on this earth that is out in green.
But I mean to go through the door without fear,
Not caring much what happens here
When I'm away: –
How green the screen is across the panes
Or who goes laughing along the lanes
With my old lover all the summer day.

by Charlotte Mew

Fly Away, Fly Away Over the Sea

Fly away, *fly away over the sea,*
    Sun-loving swallow, for summer is done;
Come again, come again, *come back to me,*
    Bringing the summer and bringing the sun.

by Christina Rossetti

Everyone Sang

Everyone suddenly burst out singing;
And I was filled with such delight
As prisoned birds must find in freedom,
Winging wildly across the white
Orchards and dark-green fields; on – on – and out of sight.

Everyone's voice was suddenly lifted;
And beauty came like the setting sun:
My heart was shaken with tears; and horror
Drifted away ... O, but Everyone
Was a bird; and the song was wordless; the singing will never be done.

by Siegfried Sassoon

Joy

Joy shakes me like the wind that lifts a sail,
Like the roistering wind
That laughs through stalwart pines.
It floods me like the sun
On rain-drenched trees
That flash with silver and green.

I abandon myself to joy—
I laugh—I sing.
Too long have I walked a desolate way,
Too long stumbled down a maze
Bewildered.

by Clarissa Scott Delany

Laurel in The Berkshires

Sea-foam
And coral! Oh, I'll
Climb the great pasture rocks
And dream me mermaid in the sun's
Gold flood.

by Adelaide Crapsey

Giraffe

When you feel better from this — and you will — it will be quiet and unremarkable, like walking into the next room. It might sting a little, like warmth leaking into cold-numbed hands. When you feel better, it will be the slow clearing of static from the radio. It will be a film set when the director yells *cut!* When you feel better, you will take: a plastic spoon for your coffee foam, free chocolates from the gleaming oak reception desk, the bus on sunny days, your own sweet time. When you feel better, it will be like walking barefoot on cool, smooth planks of wood, still damp from last night's rain. It will be the holy silence when the tap stops dripping. The moment a map finally starts to make sense. When you feel better, you will still suffer, but your sadness will be graspable, roadworthy, have handlebars. When you feel better, you will not always be happy, but when happiness does come, it will be long-legged, sun-dappled: a giraffe.

by Bryony Littlefair

Gitanjali 37 *(extract)*

I thought that my voyage had come to its end at the last limit of my power,—that the path before me was closed, that provisions were exhausted and the time come to take shelter in a silent obscurity.

But I find that thy will knows no end in me. And when old words die out on the tongue, new melodies break forth from the heart; and where the old tracks are lost, new country is revealed with its wonders.

by Rabindranath Tagore

My Own Heart

M y own
heart let me more have pity on; let
Me live to my sad self hereafter kind,
Charitable; not live this tormented mind
With this tormented mind tormenting yet.
I cast for comfort I can no more get
By groping round my comfortless, than blind
Eyes in their dark can day or thirst can find
Thirst's all-in-all in all a world of wet.

Soul, self; come, poor Jackself, I do advise
You, jaded, let be; call off thoughts awhile
Elsewhere; leave comfort root-room; let joy size
At God knows when to God knows what; whose smile's
not wrung, see you; unforeseen times rather – as skies
Betweenpie mountains –
lights a lovely
mile.

by Gerard Manley Hopkins

The Convert

After one moment when I bowed my head
And the whole world turned over and came upright,
And I came out where the old road shone white.
I walked the ways and heard what all men said,
Forests of tongues, like autumn leaves unshed,
Being not unlovable but strange and light;
Old riddles and new creeds, not in despite
But softly, as men smile about the dead

The sages have a hundred maps to give
That trace their crawling cosmos like a tree,
They rattle reason out through many a sieve
That stores the sand and lets the gold go free:
And all these things are less than dust to me
Because my name is Lazarus and I live.

by G. K. Chesterton

Ode: We Are the Music Makers *(extract)*

We are the music makers,
And we are the dreamers of dreams,
Wandering by lone sea-breakers
And sitting by desolate streams;–
World-losers and world-forsakers,
On whom the pale moon gleams:
Yet we are the movers and shakers
Of the world for ever, it seems.

With wonderful deathless ditties
We build up the world's great cities,
And out of a fabulous story
We fashion an empire's glory:
One man with a dream, at pleasure,
Shall go forth and conquer a crown;
And three with a new song's measure
Can trample an empire down.

We, in the ages lying
In the buried past of the earth,
Built Nineveh with our sighing,
And Babel itself with our mirth;
And o'erthrew them with prophesying
To the old of the new world's worth;
For each age is a dream that is dying,
Or one that is coming to birth.

by Arthur O'Shaughnessy

Song of a Man Who Has Come Through

Not I, not I, but the wind that blows through me!
A fine wind is blowing the new direction of Time.
If only I let it bear me, carry me, if only it carry me!
If only I am sensitive, subtle, oh, delicate, a winged gift!
If only, most lovely of all, I yield myself and am borrowed
By the fine, fine wind that takes its course though the chaos of
  the world
Like a fine, an exquisite chisel, a wedge-blade inserted;
If only I am keen and hard like the sheer tip of a wedge
Driven by invisible blows,
The rock will split, and we shall come at the wonder, we shall find
  the Hesperides.

Oh, for the wonder that bubbles into my soul,
I would be a good fountain, a good well-head,
Would blur no whisper, spoil no expression.

What is the knocking?
What is the knocking at the door in the night?
It's somebody wants to do us harm.

No, no, it is the three strange angels.
Admit them, admit them.

by D. H. Lawrence

Assault of Angels

The mind trembles from the assault of angels;
Running in familiar light it sees the sea,
It remembers the dark subway and the lost fields of childhood,
It remembers the loneliness of first love and the end of a summer:
These are familiar and small.

But the assault of angels is more terrible; angels are invisible,
Angels cast no shadow, and their unpredicted motion
Moves the familiar shadows into light.
Angels cannot burn the fingers: unacknowledged,
They pass unseen. No one will ever know.
Refuse them: they have no claim to charity,
To ignore them offers a key to omniscience.
Angels breed darkness out of light, angels rejoice
In things we hate and fear.

Angels are the launching of a new ship,
Angels offer to inhabit the landscape of your body,
Angels will let you grow as a child grows,
They are your enemy: they will destroy you.

And a time comes when a man is afraid to grow,
A time comes when the house is comfortable and narrow.
A time when the spirit of life contracts.
Angels are at the door: admit them, now.

by Michael Roberts

Dejection: An Ode *(extract)*

'Tis midnight, but small thoughts have I of sleep
Full seldom may my friend such vigils keep!
Visit her, gentle Sleep, with wings of healing,
    And may this storm be but a mountain birth,
May all the stars hang bright above her dwelling,
    Silent, as though they watched the sleeping Earth!
        With light heart may she rise,
        Gay fancy, cheerful eyes,
    Joy lift her spirit, joy attune her voice;
To her may all things live, from pole to pole,
Their life the eddying of her living soul!
Dear Lady, friend devoutest of my choice,
Thus may'st thou ever, evermore rejoice.

by Samuel Taylor Coleridge

Harbor Dawn

There's a hush and stillness calm and deep,
For the waves have wooed all the winds to sleep
In the shadow of headlands bold and steep;
But some gracious spirit has taken the cup
Of the crystal sky and filled it up
With rosy wine, and in it afar
Has dissolved the pearl of the morning star.

The girdling hills with the night-mist cold
In purple raiment are hooded and stoled
And smit on the brows with fire and gold;
And in the distance the wide, white sea
Is a thing of glamor and wizardry,
With its wild heart lulled to a passing rest,
And the sunrise cradled upon its breast.

With the first red sunlight on mast and spar
A ship is sailing beyond the bar,
Bound to a land that is fair and far;
And those who wait and those who go
Are brave and hopeful, for well they know
Fortune and favor the ship shall win
That crosses the bar when the dawn comes in.

by Lucy Maud Montgomery

Hellas *(extract)*

The world's great age begins anew,
    The golden years return,
The earth doth like a snake renew
    Her winter weeds outworn:
Heaven smiles, and faiths and empires gleam
Like wrecks of a dissolving dream.

A brighter Hellas rears its mountains
    From waves serener far;
A new Peneus rolls his fountains
    Against the morning star.
Where fairer Tempes bloom, there sleep
Young Cyclads on a sunnier deep.

by Percy Bysshe Shelley

Gitanjali 44

This is my delight, thus to wait and watch at the wayside where shadow chases light and the rain comes in the wake of the summer.
Messengers, with tidings from unknown skies, greet me and speed along the road. My heart is glad within, and the breath of the passing breeze is sweet.
From dawn till dusk I sit here before my door, and I know that of a sudden the happy moment will arrive when I shall see.
In the meanwhile I smile and I sing all alone. In the meanwhile the air is filling with the perfume of promise.

by Rabindranath Tagore

Ulysses *(extract)*

The lights begin to twinkle from the rocks:
The long day wanes: the slow moon climbs: the deep
Moans round with many voices. Come, my friends,
'Tis not too late to seek a newer world.
Push off, and sitting well in order smite
The sounding furrows; for my purpose holds
To sail beyond the sunset, and the baths
Of all the western stars, until I die.
It may be that the gulfs will wash us down:
It may be we shall touch the Happy Isles,
And see the great Achilles, whom we knew.
Tho' much is taken, much abides; and tho'
We are not now that strength which in old days
Moved earth and heaven, that which we are, we are;
One equal temper of heroic hearts,
Made weak by time and fate, but strong in will
To strive, to seek, to find, and not to yield.

by Alfred, Lord Tennyson

Say Not the Struggle Nought Availeth

Say not the struggle nought availeth,
    The labour and the wounds are vain,
The enemy faints not, nor faileth,
    And as things have been, they remain.

If hopes were dupes, fears may be liars;
    It may be, in yon smoke concealed,
Your comrades chase e'en now the fliers,
    And, but for you, possess the field.

For while the tired waves, vainly breaking,
    Seem here no painful inch to gain,
Far back through creeks and inlets making
    Comes silent, flooding in, the main.

And not by eastern windows only,
    When daylight comes, comes in the light,
In front the sun climbs slow, how slowly,
    But westward, look, the land is bright.

by Arthur Hugh Clough

Do Not Stand at my Grave and Weep

Do not stand at my grave and weep.
I am not there. I do not sleep.

I am a thousand winds that blow.
I am the diamond glints on snow.
I am the sun on ripened grain.
I am the gentle autumn's rain.

When you awaken in the morning's hush,
I am the swift uplifting rush
Of quiet birds in circling flight.
I am the stars that shine at night.

Do not stand at my grave and cry,
I am not there, I did not die.

by Mary Elizabeth Frye

No Mourning, By Request

Come not to mourn for me with solemn tread
Clad in dull weeds of sad and sable hue,
Nor weep because my tale of life's told through,
Casting light dust on my untroubled head.
Nor linger near me while the sexton fills
My grave with earth – but go gay-garlanded,
And in your halls a shining banquet spread
And gild your chambers o'er with daffodils.

Fill your tall goblets with white wine and red,
And sing brave songs of gallant love and true,
Wearing soft robes of emerald and blue,
And dance, as I your dances oft have led,
And laugh, as I have often laughed with you –
And be most merry – after I am dead.

by Winifred Holtby

Everything Is Going to Be All Right

How should I not be glad to contemplate
the clouds clearing beyond the dormer window
and a high tide reflected on the ceiling?
There will be dying, there will be dying,
but there is no need to go into that.
The lines flow from the hand unbidden
and the hidden source is the watchful heart;
The sun rises in spite of everything
and the far cities are beautiful and bright.
I lie here in a riot of sunlight
watching the day break and the clouds flying.
Everything is going to be all right.

by Derek Mahon

INDEX OF POEMS

U

V

W

Y

INDEX OF POETS

D

E

F

G

H

I

J

ACKNOWLEDGMENTS

The publisher would like to thank the following:
Page 20: Langston Hughes, "Dreams," from *The Collected Poems of Langston Hughes* (Alfred A Knopf Inc), reproduced by permission of David Higham Associates; Page 54: Remi Graves, "It Is Everywhere," © Remi Graves, reproduced by permission of the author; Page 55: Walter de la Mare, "Courage," with acknowledgement to The Literary Trustees of Walter de la Mare and the Society of Authors as their representative; Page 82: Maura Dooley, "The Celestial Announcer," from *Sound Barrier: Poems 1982–2002* (Bloodaxe Books, 2002). Reproduced with permission of Bloodaxe Books. www.bloodaxebooks.com; Page 86: Hollie McNish, "Libraries Exist," used with permission of Lewinsohn Literary Ltd; Pages 94–95: Cynthia Miller, "Sonnet with Lighthouses," from *Honorifics* (2021) © Published by permission of Nine Arches Press. www.ninearchespress.com; Page 98: Mervyn Morris, "A Chant Against Death," from *Peelin Orange: Collected Poems* (2017), published by Carcanet Press; Page 162: Adam Zagajewski, "Try to Praise the Mutilated World" from *Selected Poems* published by Faber and Faber Ltd and from *Without End: New and Selected Poems*, translated by several translators. Copyright © 2002 by Adam Zagajewski. Translation copyright © 2002 by Farrar, Straus and Giroux. Reprinted by permission of Farrar, Straus and Giroux. All Rights Reserved; Page 171: Denise Levertov, "Variation on a Theme by Rilke," from *Denise Levertov: New Selected Poems* (Bloodaxe Books, 2003). Reproduced with permission of Bloodaxe Books. www.bloodaxebooks.com; Page 177: Jaan Kaplinski, "The Washing," from *Jaan Kaplinski: Selected Poems*, tr. Sam Hamil, Hildi Hawkins et al. (Bloodaxe Books, 2011). Reproduced with permission of Bloodaxe Books. www.bloodaxebooks.com; Page 181: Jen Feroze, "Boxing Day Swimmers," from *A Dress with Deep Pockets* (Smith/Doorstop Books, 2025) © Jen Feroze, reproduced by permission of the author; Page 194: Helen Dunmore, "My Life's Stem Was Cut," from *Counting Backwards: Poems 1975–2017* (Bloodaxe Books, 2019). Reproduced with permission of Bloodaxe Books. www.bloodaxebooks.com; Page 196: Shauna Darling Robertson, "Dancing with Life" © Shauna Darling Robertson, reproduced by permission of the author; Pages 212–213: Alberto Ríos, "A House Called Tomorrow" © Alberto Ríos, reproduced by permission of the author; Page 217: Christopher Logue, "Come to the Edge," from *Selected Poems* published by Faber and Faber Ltd. Copyright © Christopher Logue; Page 238: Selena Godden, "But First Make Tea," from *With Love, Grief and Fury* (2024), published by Canongate Books Limited; Page 243: Kathleen Jamie, "Lochan," from *Selected Poems* by Kathleen Jamie. First published in the UK in 2018 by Picador, an imprint of Pan Macmillan. Reproduced by permission of Macmillan Publishers International Ltd. Copyright © Kathleen Jamie 2018; Page 250: Wendell Berry, "The Peace of Wild Things," published by Penguin. Copyright © Wendell Berry, 1964, 1968, 1970, 1973, 1977, 1980, 1982, 1994, 1999, 2005, 2016. Reprinted by permission of Penguin Books Limited; Pages 294–295: Helen Burke, "Tomorrow," from *Today the Birds will Sing* (Valley Press, 2017); Page 301: Matt Goodfellow, "Ginny Greenteeth," from *Falling Out of the Sky* (Emma Press, 2015). Copyright © Matt Goodfellow, 2015; Page 304: Helen Cadbury, "Ceremony," from *Forever, Now* (Valley Press, 2017; Page 321: Philip Larkin, "The Trees," from *The Complete Poems of Philip Larkin*, edited by Archie Burnett. Published by Faber and Faber Ltd. Copyright © 2012 by The Estate of Philip Larkin. Reprinted by permission of Farrar, Straus and Giroux. All Rights Reserved; Page 332: Rachel Jeffcoat, "First Day of Summer," © Rachel Jeffcoat, reproduced by permission of the author; Page 335: Siegfried Sassoon, "Everyone Sang" copyright © Siegfried Sassoon by kind permission of the Estate of George Sassoon; Page 338: Bryony Littlefair, "Giraffe," from *Giraffe* (Seren Books, 2017); Page 353: Derek Mahon, "Everything Is Going To Be All Right." By kind permission of the author's Estate and The Gallery Press, Loughcrew, Oldcastle, County Meath, Ireland from *The Poems: 1961–2020* (2021).